Touching America
With Two Wheels

VINTAGE BOOKS

A Division of Random House
New York

Touching America With Two Wheels

Vince Streano

First Vintage Books Edition, May 1974

Copyright © 1974 by Vince Streano
All rights reserved under International
and Pan-American Copyright Conventions.
Published in the United States by Random
House, Inc., New York, and simultaneously
in Canada by Random House of Canada
Limited, Toronto. Originally published by
Random House, Inc., in 1974.

Library of Congress Cataloging in
Publication Data
Streano, Vince.
    Touching America with two wheels.
    1. Motorcyling.   2. Motorcycling—
United States.
I. Title.
[GV1059.5.S77 1974b]   796.7′5   73-20564
ISBN 0-394-71053-3

Manufactured in the United States of
America

To Gordon and Gloria Grant Without Gordon's writing talent and Gloria's delicious meals, the book would have been impossible.

Contents

Touching America
With Two Wheels

Introduction

Ed Barnes drove his Ford into the small Iowa town for two reasons. He wanted to buy some groceries and he wanted people to see the FOR SALE sign in the car's rear window. He parked on the dusty street, went into the shadowy coolness of the store with its smells of coffee beans and cheeses, and a few minutes later emerged carrying a sack. He was just about to put it in the back seat when a man on a Harley-Davidson motorcycle rode by.

The rider saw the sign in the car, made a slow U-turn and came back to where Ed was standing. Straddling his idling machine, he asked Ed how much he wanted for the Ford. Ed never has been able to explain the impulse that made him blurt out: "Why don't we just trade even, straight across, your motorcycle for my Ford?"

The other man was equally impulsive: "Done!" he said.

Ed put his bag of groceries on the ground, gave the man the car keys and watched him drive away. Then, for the first time in his life he straddled a motorcycle, bounced up and down in the saddle a couple of times, and got off and walked across the street to a pay phone. He put a nickel in the slot and called his wife.

"Honey," he said, "pack a few little things together and we'll take a weekend trip. I just traded the car for a motorcycle."

He learned how to ride the machine on the way home with a sack of groceries balanced on the gas tank. When he got there, his wife was sitting on the front porch with a pile of belongings stacked at her feet. They bundled the stuff together, tied it onto the bike and roared away. The weekend stretched into eight months as Ed and his wife criss-crossed the nation three times, visiting all forty-eight states. It was 1938.

Cross-country motorcycle travel was not entirely unheard-of in those years of the Great Depression, but in most of the places Ed went it might as well have been.

"We'd ride into some of those towns," Ed recalls, "and the people would actually run and hide. They'd never seen a cycle before. But after we shut down the engine they'd come out little by little and gather 'round and ask questions."

Today there are an estimated three quarters of a million Ed Barneses criss-crossing the United States on motorcycles, exploring the back roads and the small towns, getting to know their country and its people as only a biker can in these times of air-conditioned automobiles and jet airliners.

The people may not run and hide any more, but they do gather 'round and ask questions—the people in campgrounds who are traveling by car or trailer, the people outside the country stores, the man in the black limousine in front of the Capitol building in Washington, D.C., the Navajos in northern Arizona.

This contact with people as well as with the wind and weather, the sounds and odors and the beauties of the land, seems to be a large part of what motorcycling is all about. In fact, in preparing this book I was struck by one phrase that ran like a strong thread through all the conversations I had with other touring bikers: ". . . it's the people you meet."

I began to wonder about this. Americans travel all the time by plane, car, train and boat. They talk by the hour about their journeys and they show you color slides, but I don't ever recall anyone but a biker using that phrase: "It's the people you meet."

So this book is written for cross-country riders and for those who have dreamed of touring by motorcycle. It will not deal with racing machines, off-the-road recreation vehicles or around-the-block riding techniques. It will give broad hints on motorcycle maintenance and packing suggestions and a dozen other things, but it is not a manual from which you will learn how to set the gaps in your spark plugs or time your engine.

One chapter and frequent references elsewhere will concern answers to a questionnaire I had printed up before I left on my long ride. I did this so I would have a variety of opinions, experiences and facts from motorcyclists other than myself. Those answers, combined with my personal experiences and with reports picked up from a number of other sources have been weighed against each other in an effort to give the best advice I can on such subjects as what to wear and how to ride in all kinds of weather, how to choose a bike or a campsite, discrepancies in state laws governing motorcycles, and so on.

Bikers still have a rough row to hoe in the field of public relations. It's been an uphill fight since long before the time Ed Barnes and his wonderful wife whirled off on their eight-month weekend. Popular wisdom has it that motorcycles are dangerous. They're noisy. They're like gadflies pestering the flow of other vehicular traffic. They're ridden only by greasy bums, outlaws, sex perverts, terrorists and killers.

All true, but only to the extent that the individual rider makes it true.

Dangerous? Every time any vehicle is put in motion, there is danger—whether it's a train with a thousand wheels, a truck with sixteen, a car with four or a motorcycle with two. It's up to the operator to know how capable or vulnerable his machine is. By the very nature of his vehicle, the rider of a motorcycle is more likely to be hurt or killed in a collision than the driver of a car or truck. The answer is simple: the biker has to be more careful.

Noisy? I've never been able to understand what makes some motorcyclists think noise is power. They've got a psychological quirk. They're so insecure they have to attract attention by polluting the area with unwanted sound. I hate them and I'm sorry for them. Motorcycles do not have to be noisy.

Gadflies? Only if the riders are stupid.

Greasy bums and the rest? There were a lot of them a few years back and there are a few of them now. The movies said enough about them—too much—and I'd rather let them fade back into the woodwork and get on with the idea that a black leather jacket can be worn with dignity and can appear in a small town without making anybody nervous.

The image of the biker is changing, especially among those who use their machines to explore the country. There is something impressive about a skillful, well-equipped motorcyclist even when seen at a distance: the efficiency of his packed gear, the purposeful way he handles his bike.

And underneath the helmet and the jacket and the road dust you might find a student, a mechanic, a stockbroker, a doctor, a woman. Often there'll be a family group. They are people who have combined the wind-in-the-face freedom of a motorcycle with an efficient way of moving about. Speaking of efficiency, with fuel shortages and pollution . . . well, it's a good time to crawl out of the monstrous steel and glass cage that is called an automobile and get the feeling of a motorcycle, a feeling that a friend of mine once described as "just like going swimming in the nude."

Sometimes when I'm having idealistic dreams I think of a motorcycle as the cure for all the world's ills, not just in the sense that it saves fuel and takes up very little space but because it is the perfect vehicle for taking people into often forgotten nooks and crannies of their land, for bringing people together and having them understand each other . . . "It's the people you meet."

And I think about old Ed Barnes and the three quarters of a million others (there'll soon be a million) who are out there getting to know their country by touching it with two wheels.

1 / First Day

I went to bed early the night before because I wanted to get a predawn start on my first day out, mainly so I could make it across the southern part of the Mojave Desert before it got too hot.

I was too excited to sleep well, so I was up at 5 A.M. By the time I had everything organized and was ready to pull out, the sun was just coming up over the hills, glowing in the cool morning haze.

When I began to realize that my long-awaited trip was actually beginning, it was almost too fantastic to believe. I'd been planning for almost a year, ever since the summer before when I had taken a beautiful but too-short trip up the West Coast from California to Washington. As soon as I got back home I decided that the next trip was going to have to be across the country.

Actual preparation began when I sold my BSA Lightning and bought a new 750 Honda. Then I set about fixing it up and trying to decide what to take with me and what the most interesting route would be. My primary goal, since I had never traveled cross-country, was to learn as much as I could about the people of America. In fact, I intended to by-pass most of the tourist areas and the big cities and instead visit the out-of-the way places the average tourist never sees.

As the sun got higher, it began to warm up pretty quickly. I was really getting into it—leaning into those turns and corners, getting the feel of the loaded bike, breathing that air and feeling it all around me like I was part of it. Within an hour I had taken off my jean jacket and was rolling along in just a tank top. The sun felt great on my shoulders, and I kept saying

to myself how fine it would be if the weather stayed like this for the next seven weeks.

My plan was to ride across California and into Arizona that day, camping for the night at Oak Creek Canyon on Alternate Highway 89 just below Flagstaff, Arizona. Most of the 550 miles I hoped to cover that day would be desert. I knew that people quite often get into trouble in the desert by underestimating the effects of the heat and the mile after mile of staring into that shimmering sunlight. But I couldn't imagine anything even remotely resembling trouble that morning—at least not until I was going down a winding road out of the hills near Indio and saw a couple of highway patrolmen standing on the shoulder peering over the edge of a cliff into a 200-foot gully.

I stopped to look, too. About halfway down the slope there was a semi-truck-and-trailer rig with its engine still running but no driver anywhere around. One of the patrolmen said the driver had probably gone a little goofy coming across the wastelands, missed the curve, dumped the rig into the gully and then run away for fear of the consequences.

I chatted with the two officers for a while—I figure it never hurts to make friends with cops—and took off again, not realizing that my own adventure with desert heat was just a few minutes away. I reached Indio about 8 A.M. and the air was really getting warm. I stopped to get gas, then pulled away from the pump and parked the bike to take out my map and study it. I had my back turned to the bike when I heard the crash. There was my beautiful, fully loaded machine lying on its side bleeding oil and gas.

It was much too heavy for me to pick up by myself, and I sure didn't want to unpack it, so I got help from a station attendant and we righted it. Happily nothing was hurt except my feelings. But I learned a lesson: the bike had fallen over because the kickstand just sank into that soft, desert-heated asphalt. From then on, whenever I had to park under those conditions, I put a piece of wood or a flattened tin can under the stand.

The next couple of hundred miles was just hot desert, and in an automobile I probably would have been cursing the weather. On my bike, I didn't mind at all. My dream trip was coming true and I leaned back against my dufflebag, put my feet up on the highway pegs and cruised along feeling like the

A casualty of desert driving.

Main Street, Jerome, Arizona.

king of the world. One of Arlo Guthrie's songs began running through my head:

> *I don't want a pickle*
> *Just want to ride on my motorcycle*
> *And I don't want a tickle*
> *'Cause I'd rather ride on my motorcycle*
> *And I don't want to die*
> *Just want to ride on my motor—cy—cle.**

Mile after mile those six lines kept running through my mind, and they seemed to say exactly what I felt.

I crossed the Colorado River at Blythe, which has the distinction on many days of being the hottest spot in the United States, and kept going east on Highway 10 through Quartzite, Salome, Wenden and Aguila. I liked the names of the towns but I don't think I'll ever understand why people want to live in them. They're just a main street with a couple of shops and a few houses set way out there in the desert. But it takes all kinds.

By the time I reached Prescott, Arizona, the scenery was beginning to change and get a little more interesting. I was in the higher desert now, going through country that the magazine *Arizona Highways* features on its covers.

Jerome was the first town I came to that made me stop and get out my camera. Situated on a steep hillside, this old mining site is half ghost town and half inhabited. Just recently people have begun to move back in and fix the old town up a little.

I spent an hour walking in and out of abandoned buildings and along the main street, where I met two motorcyclists from Michigan. They had been headed for California, but a short layover in Jerome had turned into a six-month stay. They were really fascinated by the place and I was beginning to feel the same way, yet I still had fifty miles to go to my campsite and I wanted to make it before dark. I left very reluctantly.

Reaching the Oak Creek Canyon campground around 7:30 that evening, I was just in time, I thought, to find a spot to settle down in before the sun set. I drove through the entire camp without any luck and was about to start around for the second time when a group of young men stopped me and said they were getting ready to leave and I could have their place. They had their car all packed, but they stayed around and helped me unload my bike, and then they donated the leftovers from their dinner. They were traveling from east to west, just the opposite from me, and they gave me some pointers on things to see and places to find good cheap food.

After they left I discovered a very good feature about the site they had given me. It was near the community water faucet. What bettter way to meet people? Sooner or later everybody in the camp comes for water. So I just watched those that came along, and whenever someone looked particularly interesting I'd decide I needed a cup of water at the same time, and that way it was easy to start conversations.

Of course, my motorcycle itself was the best conversation-starter I could want. It seems people are always interested in anyone who travels by bike. I guess they all have a little Bronson in them, and whether or not they saw him on TV, when they come upon a cross-country biker they want to find out all about him and what kind of adventures he's had and how far he's going. It wasn't just the younger people who asked questions, either. In fact, the majority were of the older generation, and no matter who they were, the conversation almost always ended with their saying something like: "Boy, you're lucky. Wish I could take a trip like that."

Just before turning in that first night I decided Oak Creek Canyon and surrounding country was so beautiful I'd spend an extra day there. I went to sleep thinking that if the rest of my trip was anything like the first day, I could expect nothing but the time of my life.

2/ Motorcycle Safety

Safety is the primary concern of all motorcycle riders—and their mothers. Safety, or the lack of it, is the first thing that pops into a person's mind when he hears the word *motorcycle,* and anyone considering taking a bike cross-country might be interested in some exact statistics on the subject.

A report entitled "Motorcycle Facts," prepared by the Statistics Division of the National Safety Council, shows that the number of motorcycles in the United States increased by a huge 453 percent in the ten years between 1961 and 1971. All other motor vehicles increased in number by only 51 percent.

The death rate of bikers also increased. Out of a total of 67,800 traffic fatalities in 1971, 2,300 were motorcyclists. The reason for this increase could not be pinpointed, but the Council speculated that varying enforcement of helmet laws from state to state, plus lack of helmet legislation in some states, "has had an unfavorable effect."

According to the report, collision with another vehicle is the most common type of motorcycle accident, and in most cases auto drivers said they did not see the cyclist. It was also found that in car-motorcycle collisions, the driver of the car was more frequently the violator of the law.

The majority of bike accidents happen on dry roads, since motorcycles are driven less frequently in bad weather (the report says) and riders of lightweight machines suffered more injuries than those on bigger machines. Young and inexperienced bikers were involved in the lion's share of total accidents.*

*Copies of the Council report are available from the National Safety Council, 425 North Michigan Avenue, Chicago, Ill. 60611.

Motorcycles are dangerous, but not just because they are motorcycles. It takes a rider to bring out all the meanness in a machine. He's the one who abuses his bike's capabilities through carelessness or overconfidence. Personally, I'm very happy to report that in five years of riding I've never had to lay my bike down. It's an indication of the ghoulishness of many people I tell this to, that they either don't believe me or claim I'm just plain lucky.

I would rather think it's quite a bit more than luck. I believe it's because every time I get on my machine I'm prepared to concentrate, really concentrate, on a few basic rules.

Remember, automobiles and other four-wheeled vehicles outnumber motorcycles in the United States by about fifty to one, and the majority of automobile drivers show a remarkable tendency to ignore the presence of cyclists. Right or wrong, that puts the burden of safety squarely on the bike rider, and his best defense is summed up in the two words *Concentrate* and *Anticipate.* The two are very closely related and I'd hate to have to say one was more important than the other, because how can you Anticipate if you don't Concentrate and what good is Concentrating if you don't Anticipate?

In many ways, your bike can be a safer vehicle than your car. It's smaller, more maneuverable, has relatively greater acceleration and braking power, and offers unobstructed visibility. If you've been Concentrating and Anticipating, your chances of dealing with an emergency situation are probably better than if you were in a car under identical conditions.

Some of the things I concentrate on are intersections, driveways, blind curves, loose gravel, oil slicks, water puddles, small animals, railroad tracks, bridge gratings and, of course, the flow of traffic around me. I anticipate, or imagine, that the very worst possible situation is about to develop right in front of me and I am ready with an escape plan if it does. There's no way of really knowing, but I'd be willing to bet that this has saved my skin more than once.

Another thing I do that might seem a little bloodthirsty is seek out all the details I can on every motorcycle accident I hear about. Like the old saying, if you know who or what your enemy is, it's a lot easier to fight him. In checking out the details of accidents, I usually find that even though the biker wasn't at fault from a legal standpoint, he just wasn't paying the proper attention to his driving.

What happened to a friend of mine recently is a good example. Someone backed a car out of a driveway and my friend hit it broadside. When I first heard about it, I figured the accident was either unavoidable or the fault of the auto driver. Later I learned that my friend was really "gettin' it on" around a corner just before the driveway and was not anticipating the hazards that might confront him.

To show you what even a split-second break in concentration can do, let me tell you about something that happened to me. I was going around a right-hand curve on a twisting mountain road when a group of bikers waved to me as they went by in the opposite direction. I took one hand off the grip to wave and look back, swerved across the center line and brushed my sleeve against the side of an oncoming car. That was the closest I've ever come to dying, and I'll never let it happen again.

On a bike, looking back is a very dangerous practice, and it isn't necessary—except for quick glances—since the development of rear-vision mirrors. A friend who rode motorcycles forty years ago remembered this little poem: "In memoriam to good old Jack. He got this way from looking back."

Along with concentrating and anticipating, it pays to know a few basic rules about safe biking.

At intersections, watch carefully for the motorist who might be planning to make a left turn in front of you. Be prepared for him at every intersection you approach, even if it means slowing down a little.

Keep an eye on the car in front of you, especially if you are driving slightly to the right and behind him. He might make a quick right turn into an intersection or driveway, and there you are.

Always drive on one side or the other of a traffic lane (the left side is better) rather than down the middle. There are two good reasons for this: first, if a car in front of you stops suddenly, it's much easier to go around him if you are a little to one side of center. Second, the middle of the lane, where you see the dark

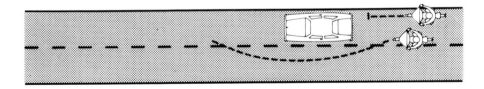

discoloration from oil droppings, is frequently slippery and is liable to contain debris.

On multi-lane roads, such as freeways and expressways, favor the side of your lane closest to other lanes so that cars wanting to change lanes won't be tempted to squeeze in with you.

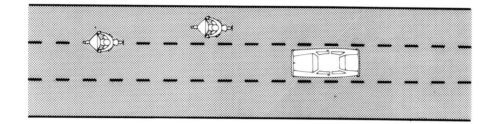

I've noticed that many bikers stick to the fast, or extreme left lane of a freeway, thinking they have to be concerned only about automobiles passing them on the right rather than on both sides. This is a good idea *if* they keep up with the flow of traffic. But I've seen some riders in the fast lane going 10 or 15 mph slower than other traffic, and that creates a real hazard when overtaking vehicles change lanes to pass.

Of course, many of the rules that apply to driving your automobile safely also apply to motorcycle riding, such as keeping a safe distance between you and the vehicle ahead, and signaling all your turns and lane changes.

In some states it's mandatory that your motorcycle headlight be turned on at all times when you're on the road, day or night. When I first encountered this regulation my reaction was that it seemed pretty dumb. After having ridden both ways, lights on and off during daylight hours, I've come to the conclusion that motorists do notice me sooner, even in bright sunlight, if my light is on. And I figure the sooner they know I'm there, the safer I am.

Brakes once were a serious problem on many bikes. The drum type just wasn't big enough to stop a heavy motorcycle within satisfactory distances. With the advent of disc brakes, however, the situation has improved immensely. Not only do the discs stop a bike quicker, but they don't fade as easily as the drums and are almost impervious to water.

Even with these improvements, you still must use the brakes on a cycle with caution. Sixty percent of your stopping power is in the front brake, but that brake is much less "forgiving" than the rear one. Try to apply equal pressure when using front and rear brakes at the same time, and if you're on a surface you're not sure about, such as gravel, ice or water, it's safest to use only the rear brake.

Night Riding Let's accept the fact that riding a motorcycle at night is more hazardous than riding during the day. You can't see as well at night, and often drivers are less able to see you. There are, though, a few things you can do to lessen the dangers:

Put strips of reflecting tape on the back of your machine and around your helmet.

If you wear tinted glasses or goggles during the day, switch to clear lenses after dark.

When you're rolling along at twilight and the time comes to switch your lights on, be sure they're all working, even if it means stopping and taking a look at the taillight. You're really asking for it if that one is out.

At night, especially in rural areas and open country, a lot of animals go on the prowl and quite a few of them cross the roads for one reason or another. If the night is cool, some of them like to lie on the pavement because it retains heat. They have a way of darting into your headlight beam and then freezing when the ray blinds them. It's a bad situation when you're in a car, and very serious for a cyclist.

It may sound cruel, but I'd advise hitting the rabbit or skunk or possum rather than risk your life by laying the bike down trying to miss him. If it's a bigger animal, like a coyote or deer, you should have been anticipating. Well, of course you should have been anticipating the little ones, too.

Generally, it's a good idea to reduce your speed at night by 10 or 15 mph, especially if you're not familiar with the roads you're traveling.

Riding in the Rain Most cross-country motorcyclists dread the thought of riding in the rain, but they know that sooner or later it's going to catch them. I hit my first spell of wet weather while camped along the Mississippi River between Iowa and Illinois. The storm had been following me

most of the day after I left Columbus, Nebraska, but by the time I reached the river it was blue skies and warm air and I thought I had outrun the storm.

I pitched my tent and went to sleep, and all was well until about 3 A.M. when raindrops spattering on the tent woke me up. Like a good cavalryman, I thought first of my mount, scrambled out and covered the motorcycle and went back to sleep, hoping it would clear by daylight. But no, at dawn it was still pouring, so I sat there mulling over my two choices: Stay put, or pack up and ride on. It looked like it might rain for a long time, and I finally decided to go with the hope of running out the storm.

I carried large plastic trash bags to waterproof the gear packed on the rear of the bike, and I learned it was a good idea to have plenty of spare ones because they tear easily if they get loose and flap in the wind.

For myself, I had a thin plastic rain suit big enough to fit over my heavy coat, but after about twenty miles of riding, the pants ripped to shreds from lashing in the wind, and from then on I rode with just the jacket. Next time, I'll find a tougher, heavier rain suit.

In spite of that small problem, this first experience of a long ride in the rain wasn't as bad as I had thought it would be, but it made me aware of a number of related hazards I'd have to watch out for.

First, if you're riding in a part of the country where it hasn't rained for quite a while, or where it has been really hot, even a light drizzle can be dangerous. The pavement, especially if it's blacktop, is porous, and all during the dry spell it has been soaking up oil from passing vehicles, dust and little particles of dirt. What happens? The first light rain goes into the pores and all that junk floats to the surface, especially the oil, and the road becomes as slick as glass. The safest procedure is to get off the road and wait for the rain to wash away the slime. The gentler the rain, the longer you might have to wait.

When you do pull out again, there are other rain-caused traps to avoid. Do not ride down the center of the lane because that's where most of the oil droppings have collected, and it's even more slippery there.

Look out for metal surfaces such as cattle guards, manhole covers, and gratings on storm drains and bridges, because they become very slick when damp.

In some states highway engineers have developed paint for lane and centerline markings that is supposed not to be slick when wet, but it isn't perfect so watch out for it. In most places those white and yellow lines are just like ice. Even when you're stopping at an intersection, be sure your boot doesn't slip when you put your foot down for balance.

Puddles in the road can be deadly. There's no way for you to know whether they are a quarter of an inch deep or whether they're chuckholes deep enough to throw you. Remember, the very same rain you've been in probably created new holes in the pavement which the road department hasn't had time to patch.

Rain deposits debris in the streets, especially if it's been a pretty heavy downpour. Branches, slippery wet leaves, bits of wood, mud and such can be expected and should be avoided.

After riding in the rain for a little while, check your brakes now and then to be sure the linings aren't wet. Do this by putting just a little pressure on the levers. If you find they feel a little slick, maintain the pressure for a few moments as you roll along. The heat generated by the friction between linings and drum will dry them out.

When braking or accelerating on wet pavement, do it as smoothly as possible. Quick, jerky motions can make you lose traction and spill.

When preparing to stop, let the compression of your engine help slow you down before applying the brakes.

And, if you intend to keep riding through that approaching squall, turn on your lights. The rain is going to cut down visibility, and you'll want all the help you can get in letting the auto and truck drivers know where you are.

Be especially alert to keeping your bike as straight up as possible on curves and corners, and maintain an extra amount of distance between you and the vehicle ahead both for safe stopping and to keep away from the water thrown up by the tires.

For me, the biggest problem in wet weather was passing trucks or having them pass me. They throw water everywhere in great misty clouds that blank your visibility, so stay as far away from them as you can.

If you're not prepared for rainy riding or just don't want to face it, or if you're caught in a sudden cloudburst that makes riding impossible, you must develop the knack for smelling out

Sooner or later, every motorcyclist is going to get caught in the rain.

good shelter. It's pretty simple, especially if you anticipate.

I learned quite quickly to identify which clouds were likely to open up and which weren't, and this gave me time to seek out a hiding place. If you think it looks like rain up ahead but aren't too confident about your cloud-reading ability, a good trick is to watch the windshield wipers of oncoming cars. If two or three of them are still moving, or if the cars are wet, it's time to hole up.

Most service stations will let you and your bike keep dry in their garage areas. Freeway bridges make good roofs. I once spent some time under the eaves of a very fancy chicken coop in North Carolina.

As I said before, next time I ride in the rain I'll have a better rain suit than the one that ripped up on me. When I got back from my trip I started checking on types of rain gear available for bikers and found that most bike shops carry suits made especially for the purpose. They come in one and two pieces, are wind-resistant and fit snugly at ankles and wrists. Make sure they're big enough to fit over your other clothing.

And about those plastic bags and baggies. Keep a few handy and slip them over your gloves and boots when the rain begins to fall. Soggy hands and feet are miserable.

Riding in the Wind
Strong winds, no matter which way they're coming from, will present some of the roughest conditions any biker can face. Riding in the rain, you can at least see the heavier sheets coming. In a strong wind, however, you must always be braced for the unexpected gust that you can't see but that can send you swerving across traffic lanes. The lighter your bike, or the higher your load, the more dangerous this becomes.

In order to keep your balance with a gale wind blowing against you from one side, you must compensate by leaning against it. But there's always the chance that the wind will suddenly let up, or you'll pass a truck or go under a bridge where the wind is blocked for a moment, and you can find yourself leaning with nothing to lean against.

The constant strain of compensating for wind changes and fighting for control every moment is exhausting. I've found that if I must ride in the wind, it's best to slow down and ease the strain. At lower speeds it's easier to regain control when the gusts or the calms surprise you.

Riding in the Snow The best advice I can give on

snow riding is: Don't. If you're at home, stay there. If you're caught out in it, find a good stopping place as quickly as you can.

If circumstances force you to be out on the road, remember that the faster you go the more uncertain your traction becomes. Therefore, as in rain and wind and darkness, slow down—only more so. And don't lean hard into corners. When the snow is fresh and powdery and unpacked, you have some chance of maintaining reasonable traction, but after automobiles and trucks have packed it down and cut icy ruts in it, motorcycling becomes all but impossible.

While you're plowing along, test your traction occasionally by gently applying your rear—not your front—brake. The rear one is more forgiving, and on slick surfaces it's best not to use the front one at all.

Just as you did in the rain, be on the lookout for iron-grated cattle crossings, manhole covers and metal bridge surfaces.

What to Wear for
Safety and Comfort Deciding on the proper wear-

ing apparel for personal protection is another form of anticipation.

Probably the most important item in your wardrobe should be something to protect your eyes. I prefer a good-fitting pair of goggles because nothing—dust, rain or insects—can get in. Some bikers like to wear glasses because they think goggles aren't "in," but I consider glasses only partly protective since things can come in around the edges.

There are several styles of masks, both tinted and clear, that attach to the helmet and cover the entire face. Some have minor faults, such as distorting vision or increasing wind noise, but most dealers will let you try out the different ones on a run around the block so you can decide which is best for you.

I consider the helmet second in importance to eye covering,

and it can easily become first in the event of a spill. Again, there are many makes and styles—pick the one that is most comfortable for you. Several of the cycle magazines have run tests on different helmet styles for impact resistance and other features and will provide you with the test results if you really want to get scientific about it. Just ask yourself when you're buying a helmet how much you think your head is worth.

California, where I live, is one of only six states that doesn't have a law requiring cyclists to wear helmets, and when I first started riding I didn't bother to get one. When my travels began taking me into other states where helmets were mandatory, I found they weren't as much of a nuisance as I had imagined they would be. In fact, on my last trip I wore one for the entire 10,000 miles and discovered, to my surprise, that now I feel uncomfortable without it.

Way up on the list of important gear is a solid pair of boots. It's very dangerous—in fact it's downright ridiculous—to ride barefooted or even with tennis shoes or sandals. If you ever need to put your foot down to keep your bike up, you'll know how good a pair of boots feels. Leather boots with metal reinforcements in the soles are the best you can get.

Many touring bikers have full sets of "leathers," pants and jackets made of soft tough leather. I highly recommend them for a number of reasons. First, leather can really take all kinds of punishment and come out looking great. You can go through a rainstorm, then let the sun dry out your leathers, and they're as good as new—if a bit stiff. About the only care they need is an occasional rubdown with saddle soap. The soap comes in a can like shoe polish and is easily applied. It softens and makes the leather water-resistant.

Second, leather is about the best protection your skin can get in case of a fall. It is strong enough to resist ripping and tearing if you hit the pavement. I once saw a man who had been riding stripped to the waist: He took a spill and skidded along the gravelly pavement on his back for about fifteen yards. With a leather jacket, he probably would have gotten back on his bike and ridden away. As it was, he was hospitalized for a month and has lifelong scars.

Third, leather is comfortable to wear. It keeps cold air out and holds body heat in. It might be a little too much on a very hot day, but the safety factor is well worth the extra heat.

Daily Safety Check

Before starting each day's ride, it's a fine idea to give your motorcycle a quick inspection.

Test your lights and horn. Check your cable ends to be sure they're not fraying. Examine your tires for tread wear or bruises.

When you start to roll, go slowly at first and test your brakes.

The whole procedure takes only a couple of minutes and can be worth a lot to you. Who knows? This might be the day you're stopped at a highway patrol safety inspection roadblock, and your anticipation will have paid off.

Just recently, while talking with a retired California highway patrolman who had spent more than twenty years on motorcyles, I asked him what was the most important thing he did to ensure his safety.

It came as no surprise to me when he said just one word: "Anticipate."

First Aid

It may seem a little gruesome to be discussing first aid in the same chapter with safety, but there are a few tips that may prevent a serious injury or infection in the event you don't anticipate as well as you should.

I don't expect you to haul this book out of the gear on your bike and read first-aid directions if you happen to be involved in an accident, but there are a few things you should do before and during a cross-country trip which might make it easier for you if something does happen.

Before you leave:
- Make sure your tetanus shots are up to date.
- Make sure your personal identification papers carry the name, address and phone number of whomever you want notified in an emergency.
- Be aware of any allergies you might have, and carry the appropriate medication. I have a thing with bees. I didn't know it until about a year ago when I got stung and almost went

into a coma. The doctor says another sting could be much more serious, even fatal, so I carry special medication with me at all times.

On the road:

- Keep a waterproof flashlight in or near your first-aid kit.
- Keep a handful of small change in the kit at all times so you won't be caught short if you have to make emergency phone calls.
- Wear a good helmet and protective clothing, preferably leathers, and something to guard your eyes.
- Wear clean clothing, especially underwear. Greasy, sweaty clothing increases the chances of infection in cuts and abrasions.

If you come upon an accident in which a victim might have broke bones, don't try to move him around. Use the money in your kit to call an ambulance. If you happen to be the victim, tell somebody else to use the money.

If the accident is in a remote area where it's obvious there'll be a long delay before an ambulance can get to the scene, gently check the victim to make sure nothing is hampering his breathing. Keep him warm with a bedroll or blanket. If there is heavy bleeding, try to slow it down or stop it by pressing a towel or wad of bandages against the wound. Avoid using a tourniquet unless you've had experience with them.

A basic first-aid kit should contain:
Some nickels and dimes
Gauze pads and rolls
Band-Aids of various sizes
Roll of adhesive tape
Antiseptic lotion
Tube (not jar) of vaseline
Small pair of scissors
Tweezers with sharp points
Cake of strong soap
Aspirin

Before you leave, make sure every item in the kit is plainly labeled. And keep the kit in an accessible place.

3/Choosing Your Motorcycle

In terms of size, weight, shape, safety features, cost, power and a number of other factors, your options in choosing a motorcycle suited to you are practically unlimited.

Your decision must be based largely on what you want to do with your bike—ride it around town, climb a hill, explore a desert, or go beyond all that and challenge an entire country with all its moods of weather, road conditions, local laws and customs, and vast distances.

For in-town riding and an occasional weekend trip, something in the 250 cc. to 450 cc. class might be suitable. For longer rides, you shouldn't even look at anything under 500 cc.

I'm not saying you can't ride cross-country on the smaller bikes, but if you do you'll face problems of safety, comfort, and efficiency that are hard to ignore. A small cycle that has to run at peak power to go 80 mph will not cruise happily at 70.

My first motorcycle was a used 650 BSA, and when I bought it I figured I'd be using it mostly for short weekend junkets, with maybe a longer trip thrown in now and then. It was especially good for in-town riding because of its light weight, and it had plenty of power for longer trips, although I found a major drawback in excessive and tiring vibration over extended periods of riding.

My longest trip on the BSA was a two-week, 3,000-mile run up the coast of California to Oregon and Washington. There was enough power to carry me, my friend Marcia, and all our equipment, but we found we could make only about 250 or 300 miles a day because the vibration simply wore us out.

Later, when I decided to ride across the United States, I knew I would need a bike that offered much more comfort, and also

In terms of size, weight, shape, cost and power, your options in choosing your motorcycle are practically unlimited.

one that had a little more power to pack more weight. I talked to friends who had ridden cross-country, and I tested some of their bikes and finally settled on a 750 Honda. I'm sure there were plenty of other bikes on the market that would have been equally suited to my needs, but it just happened that personally I felt I'd be happier on a Honda.

For long trips, my rule of thumb is that the heavier the bike the safer and more comfortable I'm going to be. This is especially true if there's going to be a passenger along, because you have not only his or her added weight, but the weight of the extra camping gear and clothing.

Overloading an inadequate bike is dangerous. It will tax your engine, drive chain, clutch, tires and shock absorbers. If you bottom out on your shocks every time you go over a small bump in the road, you're going to be nervous and exhausted before too many miles, and that's no way to spend your vacation. You must figure out ahead of time the maximum load you intend to carry, and then buy the bike that can handle that job.

Pure comfort is as important a thing to strive for as safety. In fact, comfort and safety go together, because the rider who feels at ease and rested is less tense and more physically prepared to handle unexpected situations. It's really a matter of good morale making a better rider.

The largest single factor that works against comfort is, in my experience, vibration. Manufacturers are using a variety of devices to overcome or lessen this evil. Some are going from two to four cylinders for smoother performance. Others are using rubber mountings so that engine vibration isn't transmitted to the frame and the rider. Of course, some twin-cylinder bikes are relatively free of the shakes and trembles— but a lot are not, so choose carefully.

Noise is similar to vibration in its ravages on a rider. It is a proven medical fact that excessive noise has very bad physical effects on a person under any circumstances. When applied to a motorcycle rider on a long trip, it can mean not only discomfort, but danger. Noise batters at your nervous system, causes headaches, impairs alertness. It can drown out warning horns from other vehicles, and it can rob you of the pleasure of hearing your passenger's voice.

Beyond all this, a quiet motorcycle is good public relations for all riders in their contacts with non-bikers.

Now comes the matter of your physical relationship with your bike. Test-ride any motorcycle you think you might want to buy. It's just possible that aside from all mechanical considerations, you and the machine simply don't belong together. Your legs may be too short or too long. You might have to sit in an unnatural position to reach the handlebars. Maybe you don't care if your legs are too short, but in some states, like California, the law says you must be able to touch the ground with both feet when straddling your bike. It's an obvious comfort and safety measure when you think about it.

Out on the long road the efficiency and dependability of your machine become prime concerns. It's no fun starting on a two-week vacation tour and spending one and a half weeks in some garage. The chances of this happening are fewer if your bike is new, properly cared for, and with all its weak points well known to you so that the slightest danger signal—in chain, transmission or whatever—is recognized in time to prevent a breakdown.

All new machinery has some stiffness, some kinks and quirks. Ride your new bike as much as possible before taking off to let these things work themselves out.

Used Motorcycles If you think you can save money

by buying a used motorcycle, think again. Used bikes (and you never know for sure the number of people who've used them, or how) have a habit of turning against their owners when they least expect it. It's better to save your money for a few extra months and put it on a new bike. Then you know what you're getting.

The most crucial period in the life of a motorcycle comes during the first couple of thousand miles, when it's being broken in. If the break-in rules aren't followed carefully, the engine is subject to severe damage and a shortened life, and that's about the time it goes on the market at an attractive price. With a new machine, the breaking-in is your responsibility and you're the one who'll know if it's being done properly.

There are some people, of course, who buy old bikes and rebuild them just for the pleasure of the work and the satisfaction of turning a wreck into something useful and beautiful. But if you're not one of those, and you just want to buy a bike and hit the road, I'd advise you to buy a new machine rather than a used one.

If, after all, you still want to try your luck with a used motorcycle, there are some tips that can help you make something a little better than a blind choice. Before I get into these, I'd like to tell you how I bought my first bike so you'll know how NOT to do it.

I knew I wanted a motorcycle, and I decided that a Triumph Bonneville would be my first choice. I was expecting my income-tax refund check for $900, and I knew that wasn't enough for a new machine so I was reconciled to getting a used one. Well, the check arrived and I cashed it and put nine $100 bills in my back pocket and started out.

That same day I had seen a newspaper ad for a BSA Lightning for exactly $900: ". . . one year old, excellent condition." It wasn't exactly the bike I wanted, but it was close enough and the price just happened to be right, so I went to take a look.

A middle-aged man who didn't seem to be the type who'd own a BSA Lightning opened the door to my knock. "Yeah, I've got the bike," he said. "I just moved down from Colorado. I repossessed the thing from a kid who owed me some money, and now I don't want it. I don't even know how to ride it."

He went on to explain that he'd brought the bike from Colorado in the back of his pickup truck, and that it only had 1,500 miles on it. We went out to the garage and there it was.

Dusty and dirty, still it was a motorcycle and to me it was beautiful.

I looked it over just as if I knew what I was doing. "Can you start her up for me?" I asked.

"Well, I hope so, but I'm not really sure how to do it."

So we both went at it and finally, after we had figured out such things as the gas shut-off valve, the engine sputtered to life.

"Sounds like she runs real good," the man said. The engine could have had three broken valves and a blown head gasket and I wouldn't have known the difference. "Go ahead and take a spin," he said.

I threw a leg over the seat, revved up the engine a couple of times and took off. Boy, this is great. The wind in my face. Like a bird flying through the air. I'm free. The longer I rode the bigger the hole that $900 was burning in my pocket.

I took the bike through all four gears. Or did it have five? I don't know, but everything sounded all right—except what was that rattling sound?

After a little more riding around, I took the bike back to an owner who was getting a little anxious. "I'll tell you what," I said. "I like the bike, but there are a couple of things I'm not sure about. I'd like to bring a friend over with me tomorrow. He knows something about motorcycles and if he says okay, I'll get it."

Secretly, I hoped common sense was beginning to catch up with me.

"Well," said the man, "you look like a pretty nice boy and I really want you to have this machine. Tell you what. If you buy the bike tonight, you can have it for eight hundred dollars."

I was stuck. I knew my friend couldn't come over that night to look at the machine, and I had no way of knowing whether I was getting a good buy or not. So I thought it over for a little bit and decided that even if I had to spend $150 for an overhaul, it would still be worth it.

"All right. I'll take it."

So much for common sense. I peeled off eight of the bills and I owned a bike, but at that moment I had no way of knowing whether I had made a fantastic buy or really taken a bummer.

As it turned out, I was pretty lucky. After a $40 tune-up the thing ran great. The rattling noise that had worried me turned out to be nothing more than a crash guard vibrating against the frame. But the point is, I could just as easily have gotten a bomb, and an overhaul could have cost me twice as much as I paid for the machine.

Now that I've suggested how not to do it, let's get back to those tips on how to avoid making a blind choice.

First, try to decide what make of bike you want and then research its characteristics, remembering that models change from year to year, and that a 1969 Triumph, for example, might be quite different from a 1968 or 1967. Check out the peculiarities of whatever make you're hunting for: Does it have a reputation for leaking oil? Is it an easy starter? How is it on noise and vibration? With these and a few other key bits of knowledge you can judge pretty well if the seller is being truthful when he says: "Yeah, this particular model always leaks a little oil."

Next, try to have a knowledgeable friend along with you, someone who knows more about motorcycles than you do. If no such person is available, you must have a plan—a systematic way of checking over the important parts of a bike. Above all, don't buy on impulse. Don't let bright chrome and a shiny paint job lead you to believe that the cylinder walls are good.

Okay, so you meet the guy who wants to sell and he takes you out to look at the bike. Before you even start the engine, there are several things to check out.

Go over the machine for scratches, dents, and bent foot pegs or brake and clutch levers, and for newly replaced parts or new paint. Don't hesitate to question the owner about any little flaw you find, no matter how minor, and if his answers don't satisfy you, tell him thanks and leave. A bike that has been dumped or slammed into something can have serious flaws hidden under a coat of paint, and it's too risky to buy.

If you get past these tests, go on and look underneath the engine for oil leaks, remembering that some bikes, especially the British ones, always drip a little, while others aren't supposed to.

Now put the bike up on the center stand and take a good long look at the tires. Spin the rear wheel. It should turn freely and without wobbling sideways. If it does wobble, the problem might be a major one, such as a bent frame, or only a rather simple fault, like loose spokes. Pull the wheel back and forth to check the bearings. If it rattles around loosely on the axle, it'll need a new bearing.

Repeat the entire procedure with the front wheel, having the owner hold it up off the ground if necessary.

Assuming that any flaws you've found are relatively minor ones, get down to the serious stuff. Touch the engine and exhaust manifold to see if they are warm, and then ask the owner to start it up. If your touch showed the engine was cold but it still started readily, that's a plus point.

Let him warm the engine for a while and then put it on idle, and listen to see if it sounds rough or smooth. Rev it up and listen for strange noises or unusual vibrations.

Finally, take a look at the exhaust smoke. If it's a dark blue, the engine probably has bad rings or a broken head gasket, either one of which is costly to repair.

If the bike has come through pretty well so far, try out all the accessories—lights, horn, brakes and so forth.

Now you're ready for a test ride. Accelerate slowly and listen for coughing or sputtering. As you go through the gears, does the shifting seem firm and positive? If there's any slipping or sloppiness, you'd better pass up this machine because transmission overhauls are very expensive.

If these things seem to be all right, find a long straight stretch of road and relax your grip on the handlebars so you have only fingertip control. Does the bike want to pull to one side or the other? If it does, it could mean a bent frame.

If there is no wobble, treat yourself to some curves just to see if the machine feels good to you.

A rather unpleasant but important point to keep in mind when buying a used bike is that thousands of machines are being stolen each year. The resale of hot bikes is a large and growing market throughout the country, especially in and around the big cities.

If the seller you're dickering with seems to be in a hurry to wind things up, take that as a warning signal. Make sure he has all the necessary papers—registration, pink slip, bill of sale— and check the numbers against those on the motorcycle. If you have any doubts, call your local police and ask them to make a records check on the serial number, license number, and engine number. Most departments will be able to tell you in a matter of minutes if the bike is "clean."

All this doesn't really take much time, and if you think you've found a good buy, do one more thing: Tell the owner you're interested but must think it over until tomorrow. Go away and talk over the deal with friends, or even look at a couple of other machines. Good luck!

4/Customizing

Decisions, decisions. You've already been through a few: A new bike or a used one? And if a used bike, which one? Well, there are more decisions to come.

If the bike you bought is completely stock, just as it came from the factory, do you want to leave it that way? More than likely you'll want to make some changes, and probably you'll decide on something between the extremes of stock and customized, fire-breathing chopper. If you have any doubts about trusting your instincts, a good way to get some ideas on what works and what doesn't is to study what other bikers have done and ask how their alterations have worked out. Most of them will give you honest answers about handling, safety and convenience. Since I am concerned here with cross-country touring, this chapter will take up only the accessories or customizing procedures best suited to that purpose.

A basic set of accessories for a touring machine might include a fairing or windshield, saddlebags, luggage rack and perhaps a crash bar. All four will cost you from $250 to more than $600, depending on the brand you buy. Let's look at these extras one at a time before going into some of the other less common items.

One of the most widely debated accessories is the fairing—a fiberglass shield and windshield that attaches to the front of your bike. There are many riders who will argue that they wouldn't think of making a long trip without a fairing. They claim that with a fairing wind pressure against the rider's body is eliminated and therefore he doesn't have to lean into the wind—a very tiring position—all day long. Fairing advocates point out that a fairing will fend off bugs, gravel and grit, and

Most likely, your bike will be something between straight stock and this
fire-breathing chopper.

rain and snow, and will increase luggage space since some lighter gear can be stowed up front just inside it.

Those are the good points. Now for the bad news. There are some real disadvantages to fairings besides the obvious one of aesthetics.

Fairings are of two basic types. One mounts on the handlebars or front forks, while the other bolts directly to the frame of the bike. The handlebar mounting is more popular because it is cheaper and easier to install, but also it is less desirable since the wind buffeting against its broad surface creates a pressure that is transmitted directly to the handlebars. This inevitably affects steering. It's a big force and one that you'll have to fight manually, especially on windy days. A frame-mounted fairing, on the other hand, will tend to stabilize your machine by acting like a fin, so wind buffeting won't affect handlebar control.

Any fairing, however, will trap the noise of your engine and feed it directly to you like a large reflector, And, while it may deflect the wind from the driver, it tends to make things worse for a passenger, who may find himself totally enveloped in the airstream.

On my bike, with its altered handlebars and six-inch extension on the front end, a fairing is out of the question. For a while I did try a windshield that clamped on the bars, but it didn't work. I sit so far back on my machine that the wind curled around the shield and caught me square, in the same way that a fairing affects a passenger.

But if you think you want a fairing or a windshield, test a few of them on your bike before putting down the money. Of the cross-country bikers I interviewed, 37 percent had fairings and another 20 percent had at least a windshield.

Saddlebags are probably the most popular accessories. Many manufacturers produce them in all sizes, shapes and colors. Some of the more expensive ones have quick-release locks and can be carried off your bike like a couple of suitcases. Saddlebags are so popular because they can hold lots of bulky equipment in one place and they hang low to the ground, so the weight of the load on the bike is distributed properly.

In the past most saddlebags were made of leather, but to a great extent this had gradually given way to the use of fiberglass, which is light and strong and easy to maintain. Some of the fiberglass bags have built-in taillights, which is a nice safety feature. These lights are actually better than the ones you can add to your license-plate bracket or fender because they are widely spaced. If your bags come without lights you can install a pair without much trouble.

If you buy ready-made bags, check out the mounting system to make sure they hang as close to the bike and as far forward as possible. They should be made fast in some way to keep them from swaying independently of the bike. When you pack, always put an equal amount of weight on each side and keep the heavier stuff in the front.

If you've looked at all the commercial saddlebags and haven't found what you want, you might do what I did. I went to a friend who does custom leather work as a hobby and had him make me a pair of bags. They were practical in bad weather (rain or muck didn't hurt them) and when I made prolonged stops I just lifted them off the bike, threw them over my shoulder and took them with me. They were personalized, too, with my initial carved in the sides, and they carried a major part of my belongings on the trip.

Many bikers also put a luggage rack on the back fenders to which they can lash a suitcase, scoot boot or other equipment. If you decide you'd like to have both saddlebags and a luggage rack, buy them at the same time and in the same place to make sure the mountings for both are compatible. To mount some racks, holes have to be drilled in the fender, and this should be avoided since new holes can cause weakness in the metal. Try to get racks that match existing holes.

A scoot boot is a small fiberglass case or trunk that fastens to the luggage rack. These are losing popularity because it has been found they increase wind resistance and, in extreme cases, cause front-end wobble. If you have a scoot boot, pack it as lightly as possible.

Crash bars are installed by riders who want a little peace of mind as far as their legs are concerned. The bars are usually made of chromed steel and loop around the front of the bike, extending slightly out to the sides. Their function, in theory, is to keep your legs from getting crushed if you spill. That sounds like a good idea, but just recently the California legislature defeated a bill that would have made them mandatory on all bikes because tests conducted by the highway patrol showed that the bars sometimes act as a sort of ski when the machine falls over, making it skid and spin along for quite a way instead

These two enthusiasts find the BMW both quiet and comfortable. They have added a fairing and windshield, crash bars, luggage rack and a scoot boot. If you're wondering why they aren't wearing helmets, they aren't mandatory in California.

of just grinding to a halt. Paradoxically, the highway patrol uses them on their own motorcycles. I don't know why.

If you do decide to go for crash bars, get the ones that are designed for your make of bike and be sure the mounting brackets are strong and have a minimum number of welds. I have a steel bar bolted to the frame of my bike which I use primarily as foot pegs when I'm out on the open highway. Since this bar extends out beyond the engine on both sides, it serves the same purpose as a crash bar along with giving me a place to hang my feet.

Some people, including me, believe that a customized seat is mandatory for long-distance riding. Unfortunately, motorcycle manufacturers have yet to design the one seat that without any alterations gives good support and comfort for all shapes and sizes of humans. I can see their problem. It's pretty tough to make one saddle that will serve all ends. So most of us who want something tailored to our own posterior will have to go to a custom seatmaker. Try to get a seat that is wide enough to give you plenty of support, and be sure it's long enough to handle a passenger and/or some luggage.

I also added a built-in padded backrest, or sissy bar, for the passenger. When there's no passenger, I can tie things to it or put a sleeping bag there to rest my back against.

If you're sure you'll always want to go solo, consider the kind of seat used by most motorcycle policemen. They're sort of like a large, old-fashioned bicycle saddle with plenty of support for the widest part of your seat, and they're very comfortable for one person. If you want a passenger AND one of these saddles, think about a sidecar. (See Chapter 5, which discusses sidecars and also trailers and the necessary alterations for installing both.)

If your stock handlebars don't feel quite right, especially after you've altered your seat, there's a wide choice of shapes and sizes available.

The overall appearance of your machine is a personal matter, so I'll just mention a few of the options and specialized items available. You'll notice that most of them are practical and not just for looks.

Some motorcyclists never seem to be able to get enough lights. I saw one full-dress Harley rolling down the road with eight taillights. I'll admit that extra taillights are an added safety feature, but I thought he was overdoing it just a little.

If your bike is stock, it probably has only a single taillight, and if that burns out in the middle of a night ride and you don't notice it right away, the result could be disaster. As I said before, saddlebags are good places for extra lights. If you have a sissy bar, you might want to mount one up near the top of it. Reflective tape on your helmet and rear fender provide additional visibility from the rear.

Most motorcycles now come with turn signals. Check your state's laws on these items. In California they are not mandatory, as they are with cars, but the law says if you do have them, they must be in working order.

A small custom option that pays big dividends on long trips is a set of cruising pegs, sometimes called Frisco pegs. Attach a pair of these footrests high up on the front of your bike, and no matter how comfortable your normal riding position may be, after a few hours you'll be happy to change it by putting your feet up there. Also, as I said earlier, if the bar supporting the pegs is long enough and strong enough, it'll double as a crash bar if you fall over.

For those who want to keep their machines as clean and trim-looking as possible and who don't figure on carrying too much luggage, a well-designed and attractive sissy bar is a practical option. Many custom machines have them installed just for the sake of appearance, but they are functional too. A biker who travels with minimum gear can lash most of his stuff right to the sissy bar. They come in many shapes and sizes so it should be easy to find one you like. But be aware of how it attaches to your bike. Some fit right on existing bolts, but on others it's necessary to cut away some of the frame and have the bar welded on. This makes it a little difficult to remove if you should ever want to.

There are a number of gauges that you can mount on your instrument panel to monitor oil pressure and temperature. Most bikes simply have warning lights, but the trouble has to be pretty serious before they flash on. The gauges tell you of even the slightest variation from normal. Their main drawback is that they're usually too sensitive to hold up well under the constant vibration of a motorcycle.

There are other extras for your engine, such as special oil filters, different headers and mufflers, or even revamped carburetor systems, but it's a good idea to talk these over with your mechanic and learn how they work on your particular machine.

Riders who regularly travel great distances, especially alone, have found AM-FM radios and even tape decks that will fit on their instrument panel or on the gas tank of their machines. One manufacturer is making little sets built into the earpiece of a crash helmet. With microphones, these can also be used to communicate with your passenger over the engine noise and wind. For myself, I carry a small portable radio in my saddlebags and use it only when I'm camped or taking a long break. To me, there's something almost sacrilegious about trying to listen to a radio while riding. And in practical terms, a good long Stones riff can keep you from hearing warning noises in your engine.

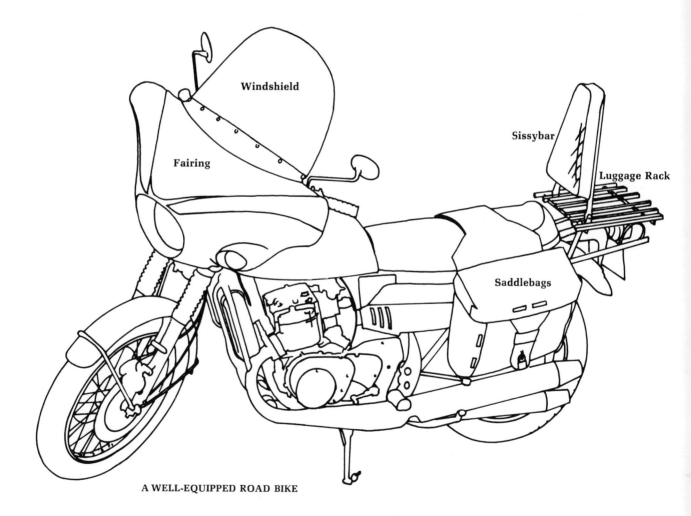

A WELL-EQUIPPED ROAD BIKE

5/Packing For The Trip

Your bike has been customized the way you want it, tuned and serviced, washed and waxed, and it never looked better—all its sleek lines poised, ready for the road.

Except for one thing. Piled nearby is all the gear you have to take with you. It's sort of an ugly pile and you wonder how you'll ever make it blend with that gorgeous machine.

The truth is you'll have to sacrifice some beauty in the interest of necessity, and while you're doing it you'll learn that you can pack more than you thought at first if you plan carefully.

Most important of all the factors you have to consider is weight distribution—and this is a matter not only of efficiency but also of comfort and safety. Every bike has its own center of gravity, and if this is upset its handling characteristics change, sometimes dangerously.

A top-heavy machine gets very hard to handle, especially at low speeds. When packing, always remember to keep the weight as low as possible. One way to do this is to use saddlebags slung across the rear of the machine. They hang low and hold a lot of equipment without having too much effect on the bike's performance.

Beginners have a natural tendency to pack everything on the rear of a motorcycle. This is all right for very light loads but not for the amount of heavy gear you'll need for a cross-country ride. Too much weight over the rear wheel puts a strain on the shock absorbers and tire at the same time that it lightens the front end of the machine, causing the front tire to have less controllable contact with the road. An overload in back also raises your headlight beam, lifting its focus point from the road ahead of you and blinding oncoming drivers.

You'll have to compensate by putting some of the load forward. This can be tricky, especially if you try to tie something to the handlebars. If one side of the load is a little heavier than the other, it's going to mess up your steering, especially at low speeds when the bike is more difficult to balance. The best place to put weight up front is on top of the gas tank. Put your sleeping bag there with some extra clothing rolled in it, and you can even rest against it sometimes when you're leaning forward into the wind. If you have a fairing, or windshield, a number of smaller articles can be tucked in behind it.

Commercially produced "tank bags" come in a variety of shapes, sizes and colors. As the name indicates, these bags strap to the gas tank right in front of you. The larger, more expensive ones are divided into handy sections to make it easier to find items inside. Some come with see-through plastic covers designed to hold your road maps. The tank bag is convenient for things you need often, and if you have the larger model it will hold some heavy objects and get them away from the rear shocks. If you're carrying heavy camera equipment, or a tool kit, it is easiest to get at on the tank.

To quickly review the most important tips on load adjusting:
• Keep the center of gravity low.
• Keep equal weight on both sides.
• Put as much weight as possible up front to counterbalance the load on the back.

In my early days of motorcycle riding, a woman friend and I decided to make a two-week jaunt up the West Coast from Southern California to Washington. I had the BSA, and all it had in the way of extras was a sissy bar. I borrowed an old army dufflebag and we started jamming all the things we could into it. As long as they'd fit, we'd put 'em in, with no regard for weight, and when the bag was full (it must have weighted 100 pounds) I heaved it up and tied it to the sissy bar with its bottom resting on the rear fender. It didn't look too steady but we climbed on and took off.

Before we had gone twenty miles I was just about worn out. The whole rig was off-balance and the shocks were bottoming

The items spread out here represent what I would take on a journey of a week or more. To see how I fit everything onto my bike, just turn the page.

out on even the smallest bumps. I decided we'd have to turn around and go home. But we discussed things for a while and finally agreed to go on, mainly because we had arranged to stay at a friend's house that first night.

The next morning I made up my mind that our load weight would have to be cut in half. My passenger's answer to this was to take out all her cosmetic bottles and dump half their contents on the ground. Somehow we got our load down to what seemed a reasonable weight and then redistributed what we had left by strapping the sleeping bag to the handlebars and putting my camera gear on the gas tank.

We finished the trip without serious incident, but the bike was pretty tough to handle because all our weight was too high up.

I've seen a number of bikers wearing knapsacks on their backs, but I wouldn't recommend it as a way to carry luggage over long distances. The pack may not actually affect your machine's handling on the road, but it will make your back very tired and sore, and this will affect your ability to drive well.

Don't overlook the little nooks and crannies on your bike as places to store less bulky and seldom used items like spare parts and small tools. I carry all my extra brake, clutch and throttle cables coiled up inside my headlight, along with spare bulbs taped together.

Flat tools, manuals, maps and such go under the seat. You can buy, or make, little brackets that clamp on the frame in out-of-the-way places to hold spare spark plugs or other items.

I saw one long-distance cyclist with a spare tire lashed to the sissy bar behind his bedroll, and inside the tire he kept his toilet articles, some cans of food and other stuff, all rolled up in plastic.

Probably the handiest thing ever invested to help a biker pack his machine is the bungee cord—a sort of elastic, stretchable rope sometimes called a shock cord. Bungee cords come in a variety of lengths and diameters with plastic-coated hooks on each end. Some, called "spiders," are double cords, adjustable in length.

Bungees are much easier to use than rope because you don't have to learn any fancy knots, and there are no loose ends flapping in the breeze. In addition to holding equipment on your bike, they are useful around a campsite. Be sure to include a good assortment of bungees in your gear, and if one starts to wear, replace it immediately. That's a lot easier than collecting your belongings from along half a mile of highway.

The luggage that a biker takes with him on a long trip is pretty much a matter of individual choice. But for those of you who may never have tried loading a motorcycle, I'll list a few items below that you will need and that will fit safely on a machine.

• For camping out and cooking: sleeping bag, foam-rubber mat or air mattress, ground cloth or plastic tarp, tent, flashlight, some nylon rope, matches or lighter, stove, frying pan and saucepan, silverware, can opener, sharp knife, large spoon, scouring pads. If you plan to do a minimum of camping out and you intend to spend most nights in motels or homes of friends, most of those things can be eliminated. But in any case I would carry the necessary items to get me through an emergency— such as sleeping bag, ground cloth, flashlight, matches, knife, can opener and spoon.

• Clothing is a personal matter, but just to give you a starting point in your planning, here are my recommendations: about three pairs of socks and changes of underwear, a couple of cotton shirts for hot weather and heavier ones for chilly days, at least one extra pair of trousers, a scarf and gloves, a pair of sneakers or sandals to wear after you take off your boots in

Well, here's the solution. The heavier items, such as stove, tools, camping equipment, are packed in the two saddlebags. This keeps most of the weight low. Lighter items, such as sleeping bag, tent and clothing are packed in the duffel bag attached to the seat. Camera gear and other things I might need in a hurry are on the tank. You can see that a passenger has plenty of room behind me, and can lean back comfortably on the rigid seat back.

camp, rain gear (see Chapter 2), cold-weather clothing (see Chapter 9), and a few towels.
• For the bike: a tool kit, owner's manual, syphoning hose, spare parts, locking device and towrope. (See Chapter 10.)
• One of the most important items is a supply of plastic bags of various sizes, including the big ones for trash. You'll find endless uses for them—protecting yourself and your things from moisture, storing food, laundry and litter, and so forth. When folded flat, they take up almost no space and can be tucked into available corners.

When you're ready to put all this stuff on your bike for the first time, try to do it with at least a little method. Spread the gear out and separate it into categories, such as camping equipment, clothing and tools. Then decide which things you're going to be reaching for most often—like maps, cameras, matches, tools, flashlight—and find handy places for them.

Try riding around the block once to check for balance before you hit the open road.

You might have to load and reload a couple of times at the beginning, but pretty soon it'll all come naturally and you'll be able to do it in the dark, if necessary.

And if the beautiful lines of your bike are distorted a little bit by the load, console yourself with the knowledge that you're a self-sufficient unit, you and your machine, capable of covering a lot of miles with no outside help.

Just remember to keep the load low, and balanced from front to back and side to side.

Sidecars and Trailers
If you want to give up a little bit of what it's all about—I mean pure two-wheeling across the country—sidecars and trailers provide some choices.

Both will give you what you're after in extra storage space and more room for a passenger. And both will take away some of the feeling of free flight that makes biking what it is.

There seems to be renewed interest in sidecars lately (they never lost their popularity in Europe) as techniques are developed for making them stronger, lighter and more comfortable, and as more and more riders want to take family or

If you are one of those self-sufficient types who travels with no more than a sleeping bag and a change of clothes, you can wrap these things up together and tie them on the seat behind you or to the sissybar. This arrangement will also give you a backrest.

friends on their journeys. Even with a passenger in the car, there is still enough space for a lot of gear that otherwise would have had to be left home.

But if you are turned on to sidecars, remember a couple of important things: First, you can't "ride" a machine with a sidecar on it; you drive it almost like an automobile. You can forget about laying into turns and instead worry about that extra wheel lifting off the ground on right-hand curves. Second, you'll find your comfortable cruising speed will be reduced by 10 or maybe even 20 mph.

There is only one major manufacturer of sidecars in the United States: Side Strider, Inc., of Van Nuys, California. Side Strider's head man, Doug Bingham, is as convinced as I am that sidecars are coming back. To prove it he told me about a picnic he threw recently for sidecar buffs. He had issued a blanket invitation to all third-wheelers and expected about thirty to show up. He was caught short on supplies when more than a hundred guests wheeled in.

"For a long time we made only one model sidecar," Bingham said, "a simple fiberglass shell with no kind of suspension or accessories. But demand is up, and now we're making two models, one with coil-spring suspension and one with shock absorbers."

A couple on an old-model BMW shows how with a sidecar, vacationing on a motorcycle doesn't have to be crowded.

If traveling with all the amenities is
your thing, you can attach a trailer
to the back of your bike.

There are a number of fine imported sidecars—notably the British Watsonian, whose three models come with convertible tops, windshields, luggage racks, and braking and suspension systems.

The price range on sidecars goes from $526 for a Side Strider to $849 for the deluxe Watsonian.

Trailers, which attach to the back of the bike rather than to the side, come in two basic styles: one-wheelers and two-wheelers. They range in size from a box-like affair about the size of a footlocker to a mini-camper big enough to sleep in.

Most trailers are equipped with a sort of universal-joint, swivel hitch that permits the biker to lean into turns almost as if he were riding solo. And though many of them have a disturbing habit of fishtailing, or whipping back and forth,

under certain conditions such as at highway speeds, on bumpy roads, or in strong winds, a common comment about the better trailers is: "You hardly know they're back there."

Trailers are made by several different firms in the United States, and prices range from around $200 to more than $500.

So if your bag is traveling with all the amenities, down to ice chests and portable TV sets, think about sidecars and trailers, but give yourself plenty of time to practice riding (or driving) with your new attachment.

6 / On The Road

Anyone who has ever taken a long automobile trip knows that boredom and the special kind of fatigue it breeds are the real enemies. Those enemies can be a lot more vicious when you're on a motorcycle.

I know that on your first day out you're going to be so excited, so carried away with that real feeling of freedom a bike can give you, you'll just want to ride on forever and never stop. So do it. Ride just for the pure joy of it.

It'll probably be the same the second day. Every breath and smell and sight and sound, every response of your motorcycle to the road and to your demands, will seem so new and fresh that you'll wonder how you can ever get enough of it and how you ever lived so long without it.

That's the way I felt. But by the third day some trace of reason began to take hold. Why the big rush? Why this mad dash to wear out myself and my bike before I'm even one-fourth into my trip? How many interesting places and people have I whizzed by?

Why can't I pace myself a little, combine the pleasure of riding with the pleasure of learning a little something about the country I'm riding through? In other words, the number of miles I cover in a day should not be as important to me as the number of people and experiences and scenes I could get to know if I just made myself cool it a little. But how?

For one thing, I learned that riding long distances on freeways or expressways was about as boring and tiring as staring at a blank concrete wall. Mile after mile of concrete, lane markers and roaring cars and trucks—I could have been in Michigan, California, Texas or New York. Freeways all look the same.

My solution was to stay off the freeways whenever possible and plan my route according to secondary roads that paralleled the freeways or at least had the same destination.

I learned that conditions on secondary roads don't always match up to their descriptions on the map, but in those cases it is possible to plan each day as it comes along, depending largely on local knowledge gained by talking to people. In the end, I know I got a lot more out of my cross-country trip than I would have by sticking to the concrete raceways.

There'll be times when you can't avoid freeways—there may not be a suitable alternate route, or you may think for some reason you want to make time. In these cases, for safety and comfort, drive strictly according to freeway standards.

Freeways have different personalities in different parts of the country. In Southern California, for example, you'll come across short sections of roadway where grooves have been cut into the concrete. These grooves, usually one-eighth inch deep and one inch apart, running in the direction you're going, were designed to collect rain water and provide better traction along those parts of the freeway that weren't properly engineered for drainage in the first place. The little grooves don't affect the handling of four-wheeled vehicles very much, but wet or dry they can come as a big a surprise to a motorcyclist. Because highway planners never concede that bikes exist, there is no warning on the roads when this particular safety feature is about to occur. No signs or anything. All of a sudden the tread on your front tire will start trying to follow the grooves. It'll feel strange and a little scary, but try not to panic. I've found the best thing to do is just go with it, don't fight. In a minute or two it'll all be over.

The West has grooved freeways and the East has toll roads; both can be a pain. The first time I came up to a tollgate was on a frosty morning in New York when I was riding with all my cold-weather gear on. I saw the signs warning me that I was nearing the gate and that I should have my change ready, but I wasn't like the guy in the automobile who could take one hand off the wheel and reach into a pocket without slowing down. I had to wait until I got to the gate, come to a full stop, get off the bike, take off my gloves, unbutton my outer clothing, get out the money, wait for the change, then button up again, pull on the gloves and finally take off. By that time, there was a pretty long line of commuters behind me, some of them starting to honk their horns.

The answer to this particular problem is to keep a bunch of loose change in a handy outside pocket so you won't have to do a striptease at every tollgate. This might be another way of keeping auto drivers from getting sore at motorcyclists.

Another thing to remember about some tollbooths, especially the automatic kind, is the trip wire. As a motorist drives through the booth and deposits his coins, his car trips a wire that is embedded in the pavement and the light on the other side of the booth turns green. Watch out for that wire—it's just long enough to catch in your spokes. And also watch out for extra-large, slippery oil deposits when you put your foot down in the booth.

A factor that contributes to fatigue for the long-distance rider is sitting in one position hour after hour, feet on pegs, hands on bars, back bent slightly forward against the wind. No matter how comfortable the saddle feels when you first straddle it, an eight- or ten-hour day is going to get to you. Try to arrange for as many different riding postures as possible.

Most touring bikers install highway pegs. If you have passenger pegs a little behind the seat, put your feet on them

for a while, which will make you lean forward and ease the back muscles. Just remember that neither of these should be used in heavy traffic because your feet will be too far away from the control pedals to make the necessary quick moves.

When I first started out, I was so excited I rode until I couldn't take another mile and then only stopped for a breather. After a couple of days of this I realized there had to be a better way, so I tried riding for a predetermined amount of time—about forty-five minutes—and then stopping whether I felt I needed to or not. I found that in this way I could actually ride farther each day and I would reach my destination feeling fresh and ready to enjoy whatever the evening had to offer.

One of the guys in my office gave me a tip before I took off. He suggested trying for early-morning starts—real early—and putting on about 100 miles before breakfast. This proved to have several good points. First, I could get up all refreshed, break camp, pack the bike and be rolling in about forty-five minutes. Smell that dawn air! Look at that dewy countryside! Watch that sun rise!

Then, just about the time I began to feel really hungry for a good breakfast, I'd glance at the odometer, and 100 miles or so would have passed in pure pleasure. On days when I couldn't follow this procedure for one reason or another, it always turned out I wasn't on the highway until after 9 A.M., competing with all kinds of other traffic. A bad way to start a day.

In the early stages of my trip, I rode as much as 600 miles a day. Soon I decided that 400 would be more like it. By limiting myself to that distance I had time to see a lot more and to visit with Indians and farmers as well as other bikers along the way, and I felt more relaxed at the end of the day.

Early in the trip I learned that my gas mileage really took a nose dive at high speeds. If I drove 60 or 65 mph, I would average between 160 and 175 miles before hitting the reserve tank. If I tried to push my average speed up to 70 or more, I was running dry after about 130 miles. So when you've been pushing your speed a little and suddenly realize your fuel is getting low, slow down and cruise gently at about 50 and maybe your remaining gas will get you to the next station.

If your bike has a trip odometer, set it back to zero every time you fill your tank. This will give you a quick reading on how far you can go before you have to start worrying about refueling.

On the road at Four Corners, where Arizona, New Mexico, Colorado and Utah meet.

But don't let any of these mundane things bother you on the first day or two of your first cross-country ride. Enjoy that feeling, the one you can only get on a motorcycle.

Everyone who rides a motorcycle automatically joins an elite fraternity and its pays to keep in good standing. In case of trouble along the road, your fellow biker probably will be the first to stop and help you.

Motorcyclists have a habit of sticking together, probably because they know they're just a little different from other people and are drawn together by a sharing of the same feelings. This clannishness started long before the days of motorcycle gangs, and it is manifested openly by a friendly wave or a clenched-fist salute whenever two or more bikers pass on the road.

People have asked me about that clenched-fist salute, obviously thinking it signifies something sinister like gang membership. I try to explain that the wave or the salute is simply a greeting between two riders, promoting their feeling of solidarity and brotherhood in their way of life.

I sometimes play a little game, trying to guess whether the oncoming rider is going to wave or raise the clenched fist, and I give the one I think he's going to give, and keep score on how many times I'm right. But whether I'm playing the game or not, I greet them all. It's one way of keeping the clan together—and I might be the next biker who needs help on the highway.

7 / Police

Policemen and motorcyclists have long been held by the popular mythology to be bitter foes. This is understandable if you think back to the image bikers had as little as ten or fifteen years ago. At that time almost every biker you met on the road was an outlaw, and policemen treated all motorcyclists accordingly.

I think that now policemen's long-held prejudices about bikers are changing, and in a large part because bikers are more and more coming from all segments of society. The

average motorcyclist today is very likely to be the guy next door or the local doctor.

In my survey I asked bikers whether they felt they had been treated fairly by the men in blue. Nearly all the responses indicated not only that bikers had no complaints about policemen they dealt with, but that in fact they had high praise for them. And I found this equally true for myself. On my trip, whenever I needed help finding a place to stay, an address in a strange town, the nearest post office or whatever, I could always count on the local police to be the best source of information. In Washington, D.C., a motorcycle cop led me clear across town to the front door of an address I was having trouble locating.

Many policemen in my hometown ride bikes for pleasure. One local motorcycle club called the "Peacemakers" was started by two policemen, and the membership now numbers over half police officers.

So if you find yourself in a strange town with a problem, don't hesitate to ask the nearest policeman for help. That's what he's there for.

8 / Navajo Visit

Above Flagstaff, Arizona, on Highway 160, I traveled through the Navajo Indian reservation, an area of arid desert where it seems as though even the weeds have a tough time surviving.

For a long time I've been interested in and have wondered about the situation of American Indians, but I'd never had a chance to make even the slightest personal observations or contacts. My first encounter with some of the Navajo people was very superficial. It happened at a rest stop in a place called Elephant's Feet, named for two giant pillars of sandstone nearby.

Three Indian girls were sitting in the shade of a big rock offering beaded necklaces and bracelets for sale. The temperature was at least 100 degrees in the shade, and when there were no customers the girls crept under their table for further protection from the sun. They were very shy and didn't talk much except to tell prices, and they got even more shy when it came to having their pictures taken. They ranged in age from about eight to about fourteen, and from what I could gather they were out there in the heat every day trying to earn a little money for their families.

I rode on, passing through the towns of Tonalea, Cow Springs, Kayenta and a few others, each one just a wide spot in the road with maybe a gas station and a small store or cafe. Every now and then, off in the distance, I would see the house, or hogan, of a Navajo family. All I could think of was how interesting it would be to go in and visit and see how these people lived their lives. The thought kept nagging at me, yet I kept putting it aside because I couldn't quite work up the nerve to invite myself in.

An Indian family living on
the Navajo reservation just
north of Flagstaff, Arizona.
The mother is weaving a rug
that will be offered for sale
at the local trading post.

But just outside a place called Mexican Water I pulled into a rest stop to let my bike cool off, and while I was looking around I saw another one of those houses. It looked as if the road to the house started right at the rest stop. I argued with myself for about fifteen minutes, then finally screwed up my courage and said, "Now or never."

The road was about half a mile long and almost all deep sand, and I nearly dumped the bike a couple of times trying to negotiate it. I decided to park about a hundred yards from the house so as not to scare some goats and chickens that were running around in front.

I still hadn't seen any people and was beginning to think maybe the place was deserted, but as I walked a little closer I caught a glimpse of some eyes peering at me between the boards of the building.

There were no doors or windows, just openings where they should have been. The front yard was littered with junk cars and parts of cars and the house looked as if it was made from whatever could be found that would hold a nail. There were no plants, not even weeds.

Pretty soon I was close to the opening where the door ought to have been, and I craned my neck and peeked in. What I saw was a scene that looked like it had been built as a set for an old cowboy-and-Indian movie. Over near the back wall was an old woman weaving a rug on a very primitive-looking loom. Seven children were all squeezed together on the one bed in the corner, and all of them were staring at me with huge eyes.

Besides the bed and the loom there was hardly any furniture, and the floor was just dirt or sand. There was no electricity. Water, I found out later, was carried in from a well out back.

I tried smiling at all those eyes, and the oldest child—a boy in his teens—finally walked over toward me.

I said hi and introduced myself and told him I was passing by on my motorcycle and had always wondered what it was like in those Indian houses I saw from the highway. The boy told me his name was Tim and that I would be welcome to stay and talk awhile.

It was a little tough to get a conversation rolling, and I felt pretty uncomfortable with everybody staring at me and not saying anything. I really wanted to take some pictures, but decided I'd better wait and see how things developed.

Little by little, I learned from Tim that the family had lived on this reservation all their lives, that the children had to go forty miles each way to school, and that their only income was from the rugs the mother was weaving. After sitting around for about forty-five minutes asking all the questions I could think of, I finally got around to telling Tim I'd like to take some pictures if it was all right with the family. He asked his mother and she said yes, so I asked Tim to come out to the motorcycle and help me get my cameras.

I like to credit the bike with actually breaking the ice with this family. When Tim saw it he really began to loosen up and start talking and asking questions about the machine and about my trip. Together we pushed the bike up closer to the house, and the other children came out and gathered around and took turns touching it and sitting on it. I got some pictures of them, and then we went inside for some shots of the mother at her loom.

I stayed around for about three hours, and when I finally left to make my night's destination at Mesa Verde National Park in Colorado I did a lot of thinking about Tim and his brothers and sisters.

I knew I could not judge all Navajo families by just this one, but I did know that they and a lot more like them live a pretty tough life by most standards.

9 / Riding Hot And Cold

Most cross-country riders will plan their trips, as I did, to coincide with generally good weather, and for the greater part of the country this would be from late spring to early fall. Even so, there will be times when a little knowledge about drastic temperature extremes will come in handy. Very soon the experienced biker will realize that in really cold weather he'll worry most about his own comfort, while in very hot weather his main concern will be with keeping his bike happy.

Since I was riding in the summer, most of my experience was with extreme heat. Most riders really hope for warm or even hot temperatures, since it's so much easier to be comfortable in the heat than in the cold. But extreme heat creates extra problems for his bike.

Heat is the worst enemy of the air-cooled engine and can destroy it in nothing flat. When the temperature gets up to 90 degrees or more, the air temperature is going to be about the same as the temperature of the engine and it's not going to cool it off a bit.

Motorcycle engines run hot under the best of circumstances, and above-average temperatures call for above-average precautions because in the heat oil runs thinner and doesn't cling to the moving parts as it should. The parts expand and contract more than usual. Suzuki has come out with a water-cooled engine, but that isn't the final answer to the fight against heat.

In hot weather, don't overload your engine. Watch your rpm and don't hesitate to shift down in gears to avoid lugging or straining. Pay extra attention to your drive chain. Heat will cause it to expand and get out of adjustment. (See Chapter 10).

Also it will need more frequent lubricating, because the thinner oil will be flung off more quickly.

Don't let your machine sit out in the sun with the engine idling. When it's not moving ahead there's no air flowing over the surfaces to cool it.

During lunch or rest breaks, try to find a patch of shade to park your bike in. It'll have a chance to cool off a little, and a blistering hot saddle might make you forget how good your lunch was.

If you hit a really bad heat spell that seems like it might last a few days, consider riding only at night and holing up during the hottest part of the day.

Operating in the lower temperature ranges can be very tricky. You stand beside your bike, ready to go, knowing the air is a little nippy but telling yourself it's not bad enough to worry about. You take off and all of a sudden it feels three times as cold as you thought it was and your teeth are chattering and your face begins to ache.

This is a phenomenon known as the "chill factor."

We all know that the weather seems to get colder when the wind blows. The same thing happens when you start riding in still air: you create a wind and it gets colder. The chill factor formula explains why.

Here's how it goes: Let's say the air temperature when you're ready to leave one morning is 30 degrees and there is no breeze blowing. By the time you reach 30 mph the temperature of the air outside your clothing and hitting your face will have dropped to 2 degrees below zero, and that's cold. If you get up to 40 mph, it'll drop to 6 below.

Suppose the still-air temperature were right at zero and you speeded up to 40 mph. Almost instantly you'd be subjecting yourself to a bitter 50 degrees below zero. It might help you to know that exposed skin will begin to suffer frostbite at somewhere around 25 degrees below zero. A leather jacket over a sweater is nowhere near enough protection. You're going to need a lot more from the tips of your toes to the top of your head.

The Eskimos have their own answer to extreme cold. They wear long loose clothing with hoods at the top to trap body heat, which, of course, rises. They don't wear anything tight to cut off circulation either of blood or of warm air inside the clothing. That theory is a good one for a biker to keep in mind even though it may not be entirely practical when he's fighting powerful winds that could rip loose clothing to ribbons.

In extreme cold, remember that your only source of heat will probably be from your own body and you don't want to let it get away. A basic rule is to put next to your skin soft, loosely woven material with lots of little air spaces in it. More tightly woven materials go on the outside. A friend who remembers World War II told me the army had a saying, "Cotton over wool," which served as an easy reminder for troops in cold weather since cotton has the tighter weave.

Because heat rises, let's worry first about keeping the feet warm. Whatever warmth they put out can help warm the upper parts of your body. Put on fluffy wool socks first and be sure the cotton ones that come next are big enough to go comfortably over them. I'm assuming you already have on long johns, and you'll remember not to put the boots on until you've taken care of the trousers.

Use the same rule for trousers and shirts—cotton over wool—and try to keep it all just a little bit loose and free.

The critical spots where heat can escape and cold can get to in to replace it will be at the ankles, wrists, waist and neck. If your boots come above your ankles, be sure that at least one pair of pants comes down over the tops on the outside, with a drawstring to snug them up. Gauntleted gloves will take care of your wrists.

When dressing for warmth, try to think of your body as a whole rather than two parts, upper and lower. Figure out some way to close the usual gap at your waist, starting with one-piece long underwear. Try shirts with long tails and overalls held up by shoulder straps.

Leather jackets that come down only to the waist may look jazzy, but every time you bend over you open a big gap for the cold air to rush in. A jacket with a slight skirt effect will be better, coveralls even more so.

For the head and neck try a knitted wool hood that covers all of the face except for the eyes, nose and mouth. If your cycle shop doesn't have these hoods, a ski shop will. The hood should be long enough to reach down over your neck, and it wouldn't hurt to have a scarf to wrap around to plug up any little spaces where body heat could leak out. The scarf can also be pulled up over your mouth and nose, bandit-fashion, when necessary.

With your goggles, helmet and face mask, and a windshield or fairing out front, you'll be reasonably snug in the cold weather.

If you're really going all out for cold-weather riding, motorcycle accessory shops now have such luxury items as gloves and vests that plug into your bike's electrical system and work like an electric blanket—when they work. (If they stop working they can do heavy damage to the electrical system.) There are also some new thermal fabrics that you might want to investigate. But as a general rule, nothing keeps you as warm as natural fibers, like wool.

One final note on the cold side. A biker who happens to get caught out in bitter weather without proper gear can take emergency action by lining the insides of his trousers and jacket with newspapers. The paper provides excellent insulation but obviously is only a stopgap trick.

Early in the trip I worked out a little game that I played with the elements. Every morning I'd try to guess what the weather was going to be like for that day's ride. I'd get up and feel the air and I'd say to myself that it was going to warm up pretty soon, so I'd start out by dressing in light clothing. But that was before I knew about the chill factor and I almost froze a couple of times. Finally I learned that it's easier to take clothes off than to put them on, and no matter how hot I thought the day might get I'd start by putting on enough clothes to be comfortable in the nippy morning, then do a gradual strip as it warmed up.

10 / Motorcycle Maintenance

In my imagination, I'm cruising along a deserted stretch of Highway 1 north of San Francisco on the second day of about a 4,000-mile trip that'll take me up the coast from Los Angeles and loop back inland and down to Arizona. I'll be going over high mountains and low deserts.

On my left there's the crashing white surf of the Pacific and a view of the watery horizon; on my right, beautiful green wooded forest. There's almost no traffic and I'm leaning back with my feet up on the highway pegs, just really gooving on the whole scene and thinking about the friend I'm going to visit that evening.

There's a strange noise and my bike quivers and I snap to attention and get my feet down on the proper pegs. In a split second the noise gets worse, clanging and crashing, and the vibration is scary. Then there's a final clank and the bike coasts to a stop and I look back and see my drive chain coiled in the road like a wounded snake.

I'm imagining this, thank goodness, and this kind of mental exercise is a form of anticipation—thinking of trouble ahead of time and being prepared for it. Better yet, preventing it. And that's what this chapter is all about: preventive maintenance for long journeys.

The one sure way of wrecking a good trip is to neglect your motorcycle. You'll get a lot of little headaches and they'll get worse and worse, and you'll break down completely—usually in some spot where help is far away. If your bike was a good one when you picked it out, you won't have anybody to blame but yourself when you're stranded, and the friend you were going to visit that night can only sit and imagine the worst.

The solution is simple. Find and correct the little problems before they have a chance to become big ones. Be a nit-picker. Let it become a habit to make frequent checks on your drive chain, cables, oil levels, battery, lamp bulbs, spark plugs, sprockets, tires, spokes and so on. It takes a little time, but it's better to lose a few minutes than to be marooned for a few hours.

It helps to know where to look for these problems. Get out your owner's manual, and then go over your bike and learn where everything is. Know exactly where to reach when you want to change a spark plug, or to change transmission or brake fluids. Look at your cables while they're good so you'll recognize deterioration when it sets in. Familiarize yourself with the battery and with the wiring system.

If you have a chain-driven bike, pay special attention to your drive chain and the sprockets it rolls over. This chain is one of the most critical parts of your bike. It must be properly adjusted and lubricated at all times or you're in trouble.

As you look at the chain from the side it will be an oblong loop—a sort of ellipse—going around a sprocket at each end, the larger one at the engine, the smaller one at the rear axle. Along the top of the loop the chain will appear fairly taut and level. The bottom strand will sag a little, and this is crucial. The bottom edge should be a little loose. To find out just HOW loose, check the manual carefully or spend a few minutes with a good mechanic. He'll show you how to get and keep the proper slack.

The mechanic will show you a couple of other things, too. For example, when you sit on your bike your weight will cause the front and back wheels to spread apart a little bit, and this will tighten the chain up. If you add another person or a heavy load of gear, or both, it'll tighten even more. The mechanic will explain how to allow for these variables. He'll also tell you to take along some spare links and a short length of chain and a small tool called a chain-breaker with which to make repairs.

Lubricants for the chain come in handy aerosol cans, but a lot of bikers prefer a mixture of STP and gasoline. The gasoline is used to thin the STP so it can be brushed onto the chain. Keeping the chain lubricated is almost as important as keeping it adjusted. The best time to hit it with the oil is at the end of the day's run while the chain and its little rollers and other parts are expanded by the heat. Then the oil can really seep into all

Regular maintenance will help you avoid breakdowns. But if you do have trouble on the road, it's nice to have friends along who can give you a hand with the repairs.

the nooks and crannies. If you lube it when the chain is cold, say in the morning before you start out, most of the oil will just be flung off and spattered all over your gear.

As an added precaution, take a moment to examine your chain every time you stop for gas or lunch or rest. It'll be hot then, and if it needs lubricating that's a good time to do it.

I really can't say too much about the importance of good chain maintenance because, aside from the inconvenience of being stranded, a broken chain can rip into your engine housing, tear a bunch of spokes out of the wheel, or even hurt you or your passenger.

Tires come second to the chain for safety and peace of mind. Start out with good ones and examine them often. If tread wear begins to show, replace them immediately. That way you may never have to patch a tube and change a wheel out on the road.

But you should learn how to do those things anyway. Your manual and your mechanic will show you how to get a wheel off (it's a little tougher than taking a wheel off a car), how to remove the tire and tube, and how to make the patch and get it all back together again.

I once rode in company with a friend, heading for a small town in Mexico, and just as we arrived that evening his rear tire went flat. Instead of getting right with it, he waited until the next morning and ended up blowing the whole day for us. He hadn't done his homework and I have to admit I hadn't either. The problem was that each time he put the tire back on the rim, he'd pinch a new hole in the tube. After about a dozen patches, he went off and found somebody who had a spare tube and who knew how to get it on the wheel.

Keep your tires properly inflated at all times, allowing for the weight of your load and for extreme temperature changes.

Clean crankcase oil, and enough of it, is the way to guarantee your engine a long happy life. Once again, go by the manual and make it a rule to check the oil level every morning, especially if you have a two-stroke engine that mixes oil with the gas, causing a constant drain on the oil supply. If you have room in your luggage, carry an extra can or two of oil. I'll say a little more about that later.

The efficiency of your carburetor, or carburetors, changes at different altitudes, but the best mechanic I could find suggested that unless you're going to spend a long time in the very high mountains or very low deserts, it's not worth fretting over the adjustments, which involve changing the size of the carburetor jets. It's a delicate and difficult job, especially on bikes with multiple carburetors.

If you're going from coast to coast, you'll be crossing the Rockies and probably some stretches of desert that are below sea level. Way up there in the mountains, at 10,000 feet or more, your bike will get sluggish and lose power. The mechanic's advice was "Just live with it," because you'll only be up there a little while. And the same goes for the low altitudes. Only remember that if you decide to stay in either place for any length of time, get the jets changed, or better still, learn to do it yourself.

Regardless of the age of your bike, it should have a thorough tune-up before you take off. You might want to have the work done at a garage, but here's a list of some of the important things:

- Check spokes and bearings just as you did when choosing the bike in the first place.
- Inspect all control cables and replace any that are worn or frayed, especially at the tips.
- Run some oil (WD40 is a good grade) down into the cable tubes.
- Replace any worn tire.
- Lubricate grease fittings.
- Inspect chain and sprockets.
- Check crankcase, gearbox and primary case for clean and adequate oil. Change oil filters if necessary.
- Go over the electrical system, starting with lights, horn, and electric starter, if you have one. Patch bald or weak spots in the wiring with electrical tape. Check water level in the battery, and be sure you have spare fuses.
- Make a test run to be sure your brakes are all right.

Chain lubricants come in handy aerosol cans, although many bikers prefer a home mixture of STP and gasoline.

And here's a list of parts that I'd suggest you take along; they're all fairly small and won't take up much room in your luggage: fuses, tire-patch kit, small tire pump, lamp bulbs, clutch and throttle cables, spark plugs, master link for chain and six-inch length of chain, a little coil of 16-gauge wire, electrical tape. You should also carry extra motor oil, especially if you're using some special brand that most stations won't carry. The length of wire and the tape will get you through most minor electrical problems. Most of the other spare parts are self-explanatory.

Anyway, keep your imagination busy, as I did at the beginning of this chapter. Let all the bad things happen in your mind ahead of time, and the chances are they won't happen in real life.

11 / Dinner With A Farm Family

Mile after mile of cornfields. I had never seen so much corn in all my life. It seemed it would never end. Nebraska, the Corn Husker State, and no wonder!

And people live there in those houses with nothing but corn stretching to the horizon in all directions. It was hard for me, coming from California, where there are mountains, ocean, deserts, all kinds of variety, to imagine not getting pretty bored. What did they do to break the monotony, for recreation? What was their everyday life like? My curiosity grew and grew the more I thought about it, and pretty soon I found myself in the same dilemma I was in with the Indians back in Arizona, trying to work up nerve enough to stop and knock on a door and intrude on a family's privacy.

I had been more or less following Highway 80 out of Denver but whenever possible using Highway 30, which parallels 80 and formerly was the main road. Highway 30 was excellent for motorcycling—uncrowded and with enough variety of scenery to make the ride interesting.

About thirty miles outside of Columbus, Nebraska, I started thinking about calling at a farmhouse. Between getting up my courage and trying to pick out a suitable one, I covered another ten miles before I saw a place that looked like the stereotype of all Midwestern farms: a two-story white house set well off the road next to a big barn, and cornfields as far as the eye could see.

I parked at the end of the driveway and studied the layout for about fifteen minutes before I could summon the nerve to drive on up to the house. I took my time parking, getting off, and removing coat, helmet and goggles, all the while hoping that someone would come out and start a conversation so I wouldn't have to go up and bang on the door. But nobody showed and there was nothing left to do, so I started toward the house. Just before I could rap on the door, it swung open and a girl about thirteen stuck her head out and said hello.

I said hello and asked if her father was home, and she said he wasn't but her mother was.

"Good. Could I talk to her?"

The girl led me through the living room to the kitchen, where her mother was preparing dinner. It was one of those huge rooms, kitchen and dining area together, all bright and cheerful and homey. The odors coming from the stove were wonderful.

The woman looked over her shoulder and smiled and I introduced myself and sort of blurted out that I was making a motorcycle trip from California, that I had never been on a Midwestern farm, and I wondered what life was like out here on the plains of Nebraska. I suggested that if her husband was around, maybe he could take me on a quick tour of the place and we could talk for a while.

She said her husband was still out in the fields but that I was welcome to sit down and wait for him. She put me at the table and offered me sweet rolls and milk. Then she busied herself around the kitchen again and I had a chance to study her. She certainly didn't match up with my preconception of what a farm wife would look like. She appeared to be in her mid-thirties—small, dark-haired and very attractive.

In a few minutes we both began to feel a little more at ease and we started chatting. She and her husband and four children had moved to the farm from Columbus four years earlier. They didn't own the property but ran it for someone else. And though corn was the chief crop, they also raised hogs.

After a while she said something that took me by surprise. She admitted she really was unhappy on the farm and wished she and her family could move back to Columbus. She said she felt so far away from everything—all her friends were in town and she very seldom had a chance to go anywhere.

While she was talking I began to get the feeling that she actually felt trapped, and that she had nothing much to look forward to except raising children and doing housework for years to come.

I had been there about an hour when she asked if I'd like to stay for dinner. She must have noticed me drooling at the good smells, and besides I guess she didn't have much choice—what with dinner just about ready and her husband due in any minute. While she was putting the food on the table I began getting a little apprehensive about what her husband would think when he drove up and saw my "chopper" sitting in his driveway. I remembered stories about "those rednecks in the Midwest who carry shotguns in the back of their pickups."

We were just about to start eating when one of the girls yelled, "Here's Daddy," and my heart went up into my throat. I figured he would see the bike and think some outlaw rider was in the house raping his wife and stealing his valuables, and he would probably come charging in with his shotgun loaded and cocked. I heard his truck door slam and then his heavy footsteps coming to the back door. At least he wasn't running. I really didn't know what to expect, and the closer he got the faster my heart beat. And then, after what seemed like a long time, the door burst open, and in walked one of the nicest guys I met on the entire trip.

All through dinner he asked me more questions than I could ask him. He wanted to know all about life in California and what the "hippies" were like. He just couldn't believe that of all the farms in the Midwest, I had picked his to visit. After dinner he took me out in his pickup for a tour of the farm, and told me that he grew corn because it was easy to harvest, and that hog-raising was just a sort of hobby. He summed it all up by telling me how much he loved the farm and hoped he could spend the rest of his life working the soil.

I tried to reconcile this with what his wife had told me, but then I figured that they were both such swell, intelligent people that they'd work things out, and that they both had their rights to their individual feelings and respected each other for them. The more I thought about it, the more I remembered that darn few families anywhere—not just on Nebraska farms—have identical dreams.

On the way back to the farmhouse he said that someday he'd like to travel, but that he wasn't sure when he'd get the chance. It was just about getting dark when I said goodbye and headed for Columbus, where the woman had said she'd like to go.

12 / Camping Out

For me at least half the pleasure in a long motorcycle trip, half the feeling of getting away from it all, comes from camping out. You're not shut up inside four walls. You do things for yourself with a minimum of equipment, bolstering your pride in self-dependence. You meet people who are traveling like you are. You're out of doors.

I'm not alone in this feeling for camping—77.6 percent of the bikers who answered my survey said they preferred making camp to holing up in a motel.

Of course, you have to prepare ahead of time to camp out, and that means having an idea of what sorts of places you intend to stop in and knowing how to use the gear that you've packed. (See Chapter 5.)

Many bikers prefer United States Forest Service campsites because generally they are located in more natural settings and are less stringent on petty rules and regulations, which in some camps, especially privately operated ones, are carried to ridiculous extremes. USFS sites are indicated on most road maps but more complete information can be had by writing the Bureau of Outdoor Recreation, Box 7763, Washington, D.C., 20044.

Parks maintained by the various states are also shown on maps, and privately owned sites are advertised along the road. In your preliminary planning you should try to allow for relatively early stopping times, something like around 4 P.M. or shortly after. In the summer, campgrounds are liable to be crowded and an early arrival will help assure you a good spot. If you're lucky and have some choice, go for a level space big enough for your bike and your tent and not too far from toilets and water faucets. Avoid gullies and other places that might flood if it rains during the night. Being under a tree can help both for shade and for limbs to tie things to.

As for your gear, there are some things you should know about how to choose it and use it, especially the tent, the ground cloth and the tarp. When buying these items it's a good idea to go to stores that cater to back-packers. Motorcyclists owe a lot to this growing number of outdoors people for the development of lightweight efficient gear: two-man tents that can weigh as little as six pounds, stoves, sleeping bags and foldable odds and ends that are ideally suited to the limited cargo-carrying capacity of a bike.

Tents come in an amazing number of styles, sizes, shapes and weights. Primarily they are made of three kinds of material: tightly woven cotton, nylon, and plastic-covered nylon. Some are designed to be bug-proof, some have double-thickness floors. There's even one called a tube tent, a large plastic tube supported by a rope strung through it, but it leaves you with two open ends and I don't recommend it.

Naturally you want your tent to be as nearly waterproof as possible. If you're buying cotton, make sure it's tightly woven, something like 150 threads or more to the inch. The biggest problem with single-wall cotton tents comes from what is known as capillary leakage. I didn't learn about this until I experienced it once. What happens is that moisture on the outside, even if it's only dew, leaks through as soon as you touch or brush against the inside. If some item of gear, like the edge of your sleeping bag, is touching the inside, moisture will seep in. The same is true of plain nylon, only more so.

So let's consider the plastic-coated nylon material. It holds out the rain, there's no capillary leakage and it folds small. But it too has a serious problem, condensation, which comes largely from the moisture in your own body. When it rains it's worse because the warm air inside the tent condenses more readily as the air on the outside is cooled by the shower.

All things considered, I prefer the cotton tent—even though it's heavy—because there are ways of overcoming the capillary action.

Some cotton and nylon tents come with a fly-sheet, a waterproof plastic sheet which literally gives you a tent over your tent with air space in between. If your tent doesn't have one, use the lightweight tarp that you packed with the tent and ground cloth. Stretched out just above your tent, made fast to tree limbs or whatever is handy, it'll keep you dry and also serve as insulation against the sun's heat. If your tent does have a fly-sheet, use the tarp to cover your bike or to spread over your cooking area.

Try to pitch your tent so it faces away from prevailing winds, if there are any. Unroll your ground cloth, pad and sleeping bag inside, and store your toilet articles and cameras and such. Set out the food you intend to fix for supper and put the rest away, high up in a tree if you're in areas with prowling wildlife. In other words, get your camp as completely set up as possible before roaming off to look at the sights and meet the people. If you don't, you're liable to find you've become so involved in landscapes or new friends that you'll by trying to cook and get ready for bed in the dark.

A last word about the tent. If it's new to you, practice setting it up at home and learn how to repack it. Who wants to sit

With the trend toward smaller and lighter equipment, it is easy to carry everything you'll need for a camping vacation on your bike.

around a campground reading directions and looking dumb with a lot of strangers staring at him?

Your ground cloth, like your spare tarp, can have a number of uses in addition to its prime purpose, which is to protect you and your sleeping bag from the cold damp earth. It can cover your bike and gear in a rainstorm; it can be wrapped around you and your bedroll if you don't feel like pitching your tent one night. Both the ground cloth and the tarp take up very little space when packed carefully.

There are sleeping bags and bedrolls, the latter as simple a thing as a couple of blankets, the former a down- or fiber-filled luxury item that could cost as much as $150. I used an army-surplus mummy bag filled with down, which provides the best insulation, is very light and compresses into a neat package. But down can be the most costly, and if it is too expensive for your means try a bag lined with Dacron, unless you plan to spend some time sleeping out in very cold weather.

Another quality of a good sleeping bag is its ability to handle your body moisture without getting soggy and sour. A really good bag will "breathe" enough to absorb your perspiration and pass it to the outside. But even so, your first act in the morning should be to open up your bag and let it air and dry while you're doing your other camp-breaking chores.

If you are traveling two up, you might want to buy a pair of bags that can be zipped together. Whatever type of bag or bedroll you use should be carefully wrapped in canvas or plastic when packed on your bike to protect it from sudden showers on the road.

Most of us find the ground pretty uncomfortable to sleep on, so think about an air mattress or a foam rubber pad to go between you and the hard places. If you decide on an air mattress, get a good one that won't be easily punctured and allow time for inflating it before you turn in and deflating it in the morning. My survey showed that very few bikers, only 10.3 percent, wanted to hassle with inflatable mattresses, and the same was true with me. I settled for a foam rubber pad, which gave me good insulation and protection from twigs and pebbles but didn't have to be blown up every time I used it. It was easy to pack, just rolled up inside my sleeping bag. The one drawback was it could absorb a lot of water, but I got around that by getting a thin plastic cover for it.

There's one other thing that could be taken along as a sort of change of pace for sleeping: a hammock. There are some on the market now made of nylon netting that can be folded into an eight-ounce ball not much bigger than a baseball. Find a couple of trees and let yourself rock in the breeze.

Serious campers should carry some kind of stove. Many camps provide barbecue facilities or fire rings, but you can't always count on them. And fireplaces use wood, which, with the increasing number of people using campsites nowadays, is in short supply. Have you ever been in a wooded campsite where all the trees are stripped of branches up to about six feet off the ground?

Again, thanks to the back-packers for coming up with good, lightweight gear. Two-burner stoves are now available that can be folded into small packages. I carried a one-burner stove of Swedish make that measured only five inches square and three inches high when packed. I was amazed at what could be done with it. In addition to such simple things as boiling water, heating coffee or a can of soup—or anything in a can, like spaghetti, stew or vegetables—I cooked hamburgers one night just to see if I could do it. I'm not much of a hand in the kitchen, but I'm sure someone with just a little imagination could turn out a real meal on one of these one-burner stoves.

An additional advantage of these stoves is that they run on white gas. If you run your bike on lead-free gas, you can just tap your tank for an extra supply.

A can of Sterno is probably the smallest and simplest cooking facility, but you must be patient because the heat of the flame is not very intense. I met two bikers traveling together who told me they had been camping out and cooking all their meals every night for two weeks using two cans of Sterno.

My suggestion is that you visit a sporting goods or hardware store and check out the types and sizes of stoves available, or else talk to friends who have done some camping. There are just too many varieties to discuss here.

The same is true with lanterns, but whether they are the gas-burning type or are powered by batteries, I consider them too bulky for the amount of good they do. One or two good flashlights should be sufficient.

Food supplies for camping by motorcycle could include dehydrated products that can be found in back-packing shops and that range from omelets to vegetable stews to hot biscuits.

One disadvantage of these is that even the smallest packets are usually made to serve three or four people, so if you're solo you'll have to learn to use them a little at a time in order to avoid throwing away what you can't eat. There are a few necessities you can carry along without worrying about spoilage, like vegetable oil for cooking, a couple of potatoes, powdered fruit juices and instant coffee.

Of course, if you're traveling with a trailer or sidecar your capacity for luxuries is increased quite a bit. Like the man from California who answered my survey: He towed a Calafia Road Runner trailer loaded with everything from folding chairs to two two-burner stoves, suitcases and a portable television set.

Quite a few people have proved that entire families can travel and camp out by motorcycle. A man, his wife and two children did it, using two machines, a bit of selectivity as to gear, and limiting themselves to short days of not much more than 100 miles. (For further details on the possibilities of multiple travel, see Chapter 5.)

There's one more advantage to camping out: It's economical. The average campsite will cost between $2 and $3 a night, compared to $10 or more for a room. I recently talked to two cross-country bikers from Wisconsin who said they had yet to pay for a campsite. I don't know how they did it for sure, unless they smiled a lot at Rangers.

Sometimes you'll be tempted or maybe forced by circumstances to spend a night along the road or off in a field somewhere. If you do, try to conceal yourself and your bike from passing traffic to avoid being disturbed by curious people or, worse, by someone who sees an opportunity for some skulduggery. It's best, of course, to ask permission from the owner of the field—if he appears to be anywhere around.

Wherever you camp, be sure you leave the site cleaner and neater than it was when you arrived. The rest of the world will get a better impression of bikers.

13 / Two Up

Just because a person can't actually operate a motorcycle doesn't mean that he or she doesn't like riding on one, and on the open road you see more and more passengers tucked up there behind the driver.

Most of them look happy as larks, leaning back against the bedroll or sissy bar, heads turning this way and that to feel the wind and pick up on the smells and beauty of the countryside.

Most of them are women, wives or friends of the biker. Quite often it's another man, occasionally both driver and rider are women, and once in a while the woman is doing the driving for her husband or friend.

No matter what the arrangement, two people on one motorcycle on a long trip presents problems that the solo driver doesn't have to think about—extra gear and clothing, extra weight on the machine, and the important question of compatibility in a really tight little environment all day long, day after day.

I've never traveled with another man as passenger; on all my trips I've been either alone or with a woman friend. I think the same is true with most touring bikers, so most of what I'll have to say about personal experiences with two up will be on the basis of male driver and female passenger. In the end, everything I learned would apply to any combination of sexes.

To begin with, you've got togetherness in a very basic way, and it should start long before you both climb on and head for the faraway places.

It should start when you and your prospective passenger are sizing each other up for personality traits, physical durability and such intimate characteristics as cleanliness and food preferences. It should carry on when you are faced with the seemingly insignificant moment when, after just a couple of hours on the road, your passenger begins to complain and wants to stop for a rest. That's when you have to remember that she, or he, can get pretty tired looking at the back of your helmet and finding it difficult to stretch and change positions.

That's when you realize that you won't be able to make as many miles per day as a solo rider does, because when your passenger gets tired you're going to have to stop whether you want to or not just to preserve tranquillity.

But there are advantages, some of them measurable and some that just can't be given a tag or a rating. How can you put a value on the sharing of a beautiful view, or on the smell of a recently plowed field, or a sudden cooling of the breeze on your face, or a serious adventure or a funny incident?

But to get to the measurable advantages: I learned, for example, that making camp at night was much easier when my friend Marcia was with me. The work was cut in half and each half was more pleasant because we could laugh and joke and talk. Of course, I had to make room for more food in packing the bike, but the logistics of food supply actually was simplified with two people.

For instance, when riding alone I found I couldn't buy groceries in small enough quantities to be used up in one or two meals without having something left over. Who's going to sell you a few slices of bread? You have to buy a whole loaf. How do you pack two or three eggs on your bike so they won't break? With two people you can get a half-dozen in a sturdy carton and not worry about their breaking or spoiling before they're eaten.

Besides, I don't like to cook and eat alone, and the result was, when riding solo, I'd end up just snacking instead of eating a meal. After a few days or weeks that becomes a bore and furthermore, doesn't do too much for the health of a person who is leading the active life of a long-distance rider.

With someone along, preparing meals in camp actually became a pleasure, and two can eat cheaper that way than one in a restaurant.

What it all boils down to is that there are advantages to two-up travel and there are advantages to solo riding. If you're the kind of person who doesn't like to be alone, but at the same time has trouble meeting new people, then by all means find a compatible passenger. Not only will you have his or her companionship, but for some reason or other it seems to be easier for a couple to pick up conversations with strangers than it is for a loner.

On the other hand, I know that when I was traveling alone I sort of spread my wings and did a lot of things I wouldn't have done with a partner, and I had some valuable experiences that I would have regretted missing.

In the end, the best I can say is to try traveling both ways because they're both good.

14/Is The South As Bad As They Say?

Marcia and I pulled up at a stoplight in front of the Capitol Building in Washington, D.C. In the lane next to us a black Cadillac limousine stopped. It had those special license plates on it and the people inside were all dressed in dark suits and ties.

I was looking at them, trying to imagine who they could be— Senators, Cabinet members—when the man nearest me in the back seat rolled down the window and asked:

"Did you ride that thing all the way from California?"

"Sure did," I answered.

"Boy, that's unbelievable," he said. "But let me give you a tip. Don't ride through Louisiana."

The light turned green and the car pulled away with the men in dark suits all chuckling and me not feeling too happy about the journey I was just about to make into the South.

While planning the itinerary for my cross-country trip I faced a tough decision. Should I travel through the South? On one hand, I had visions of Spanish moss, lush woodlands, flowing rivers, historic battlefields, ham and grits for breakfast and sleepy little towns with people just shuffling along, never in a hurry.

But on the other hand I had heard some sinister rumors about how motorcyclists—and "oddballs" in general—were treated in the Deep South. The more questions I asked the more worried I became. One friend actually gasped in horror at the thought.

"You're going through the South on a motorcycle? Don't do it. Some of those hillbilly boys are meaner than snakes and they don't like our kind. They might even kill you. I knew a guy who was riding through a small town in Alabama and he went through a crosswalk just as a woman was stepping off the curb. A cop pulled him over and fined him on the spot, and when he couldn't pay they threw him in jail and they hooked his bike to a tow truck and just dragged it off to the impound yard."

Such stories seem to be common among bikers, like the ones about being run off the road by trucks or taken up in the hills and having your long hair shaved off, or getting beat up and having your bike torn apart. And that movie "Easy Rider" didn't exactly improve the image.

One thing I did notice was that when I tried to pin down some of the storytellers, to authenticate the rumors, they began to get pretty vague and often admitted they had picked up their information third or fourth hand, along with the exaggerations that grow like weeds when a story is told over and over. In fact, as the tales I heard got more and more outrageous, I became more and more determined to go through Dixie and find out for myself just what the situation was.

And am I ever glad I did! My biggest regret of the entire trip is that I didn't have time to stay longer in the South.

My friend Marcia met me in Washington to make the cross-country return trip to California with me. Out of the city we got on the Blue Ridge Mountain Parkway and stayed on it through Virginia, North Carolina and into Tennessee, where it ends at the Great Smoky Mountain National Park. This road is absolutely too much, the most picturesque and beautiful of any I encountered during the entire ride across the United States. It loops and swings through the length of the Blue Ridge Mountains with never a gas station or a motel or a signboard or any other similar blot on the scenery, which means you have hundreds of miles of unspoiled nature to travel through.

When you do need gas or a rest stop, you just turn off the parkway and ride into one of the small towns which are usually two or three miles away. I found these little villages and towns so interesting that several times I stayed off the parkway for a while to ride through a few of them.

Just on the other side of the Great Smoky National Park there's the small town of Gatlinburg. My advice is if you ever get anywhere within a hundred miles of it, take the time to ride in. It's just beautiful. I was told the best time there is in late October when the leaves are changing. Unfortunately, we were a little early.

After Gatlinburg we went to Knoxville and then headed south through little places like Madisonville, Tellico Plains, Farner, Ducktown and Copperhill.

All through this part of Tennessee I made a point of going out of the way to visit small towns, and while I had found it really difficult to meet people in the larger cities it was just the opposite in the smaller ones. I got the feeling I was picking up at least some of the true flavor of the South, and for this reason all our overnight stops were in towns and villages rather than cities.

The people in such places were especially friendly and seemed to go out of their way to make Marcia and me

comfortable. We never heard a harsh word, and I believe our own attitude might have had a lot to do with this. Sometimes when we rode into a town we'd get an inquisitive stare or even a hostile look or two, but we didn't give the people a chance to form a bad opinion of us. We would turn on big, friendly grins and show genuine interest in things they said, and do our best to be courteous and respectful. If there were any hints of hostility on their part, we could just see them melting away.

I think the fact that Marcia was with me might have helped. When people see a couple ride into town on a motorcycle they are less likely to get paranoid than if three or four guys come through on bikes.

The South is just too fantastic a part of this country to miss because of a few rumors and bad stories that most often are untrue. The scenery is superb, and if you're into that sort of thing history oozes out all over with Civil War battlegrounds, monuments, plantations, old town squares and those huge ancient oak trees bearded with mysterious Spanish moss. The life style and food of the small Southern towns can't be found anywhere else.

While you may not be happy with the big cities down there, as I wasn't, you should make an exception for New Orleans. It's one of a kind, and nothing I can say will come anywhere near describing it.

Spring and fall are undoubtedly the South's best times for weather. Winters can even bring snow and frost to Dixie and it feels colder than a Northern winter although it really isn't.

Summers are something else.

Temperatures rarely reach 100 degrees or more, as they so often do in the plains and deserts and some valleys—especially in Southern California. But the air is humid, laden with moisture, and this seems to intensify the heat or at least make it more uncomfortable, just as it does the cold in the winter.

In summer you'll perspire a lot, but you'll notice that if there's any breeze at all, whether you're moving along on your bike or just sitting in the shade of a tree, perspiration evaporates. In these circumstances you'll be a lot more comfortable in a light cotton shirt than in some synthetic material which tends to stick to your skin when you're damp.

Muggy atmosphere is a breeding place for rain showers and thunderstorms, and quite often you get hit with sudden squalls of torrential rain, lightning and winds that sometimes reach

City traffic in New Orleans' old French Quarter.

hurricane force for a few moments. (Hurricane force starts at 73 mph and goes on up.) The only way to cope with these squalls is to run for cover before they get you. This means you should start looking for shelter any time you see a build-up of low, dark clouds on the horizon, sometimes topped by a towering white thunderhead cloud.

Not every thunderhead you see is going to come right at you, so there'll be times when you take cover and nothing happens. But when it does happen it comes fast and is mighty vicious, so you'll be glad you got in out of it.

The good thing about these squalls is that they go away almost as quickly as they come, and they leave the air fresh and soft. But watch out for puddles that might be deeper than they look, and for branches and other debris in the road.

From Tennessee we rode through a corner of Georgia and into Alabama, Mississippi and Louisiana (in spite of the man in Washington) and finally to Houston, where we had friends to visit.

I think I've already given the impression that Tennessee was my favorite state in the South, but Alabama ran a close second. The people were fine everywhere, yet I must say Louisiana, when I was there in the early fall, was a little uncomfortable to ride through on a motorcycle. Too many bugs. Maybe that's what the man was talking about. I had to stop every few miles to clean off my face mask and I've heard that later in the summer they're even thicker. I guess if a biker hits any of the lush Southern states with all their farms and open country at the right—or wrong—time, he'll meet a lot of insects. Have you ever seen the radiator of a car that has just driven through Florida?

From my experiences, then, I'm convinced that with a few exceptions the unpleasant stories about the South have been blown up out of proportion. I made it with no distasteful incidents—and I hadn't even had my long hair cut before the trip, as some friends had warned I'd better do.

15/Women And Motorcycles

As far as I can determine, about 7 percent of all cross-country motorcycle riders are women, and age is no more a controlling factor than it is with men.

My survey turned up a twenty-three-year-old whose longest trip so far was 250 miles, and there's a fifty-two-year-old who is nearing the 35,000-mile mark and is planning her latest journey: a ride from California to New York.

Only one small item or trait which women seem to have in common and which sets them apart from men riders is that they carry very few tools and spare parts, and, too, readily accept help when it's needed. This holds true, too, for a woman named Jan Gallagher who has ridden all the way around the world and up and down North and South America, and who, incidentally, has a way of packing her bike that makes my chapter on that subject seem academic, or moot, or something.

The survey also indicates that women think of themselves not as "something special" just because they're bikers, but only as women who are not easily panicked by threat of storm or grease or dirt or worse; they've found that the payoff in freedom and fresh air, new scenes, new friends and new experiences is worth all that. As one of them put it: "Be just a bit level-headed and not too super-easily freaked out."

As for other sinister thoughts about a lone woman traveling in strange places, my questionnaire, which I gave to men and women alike, had one question which could have opened up the floodgates on the subject of what can happen to a woman alone on a bike. It asked: "What are some of the more interesting experiences you've had while riding?"

But nothing sordid showed up. Just the opposite. Jeanne M.

Uraskevich of Blasdell, New York, wrote: "Met a lot of interesting people. Have seen a lot of things that I've never paid attention to before."

Kathy Flemming, thirty, of New Orleans, talked about the "great people I met in camp grounds who were not bikers," and about "the guy who stopped, took me all the way across town in New York to get a clutch cable, and installed it."

And Freeda M. Fairbanks, who was fifty-two years old and had been riding for two years when she filled out the questionnaire, wrote: "I seem to find all kinds of silly but fun adventures. One full moon-lit night last summer I was riding along Palos Verdes East road by Marineland in California. Stopped to look at the ocean. Then couldn't kick bike starter. Two a.m., no one about. Custodian of Marineland gave me a cot in the emergency room and I slept until light, listening to the porpoises talk to one another."

Jan Gallagher, of course, is something else. She's been in so many states and countries and faced so many situations that it would be impossible to capsulize her experiences.

Like most other women bikers, she carries a minimum of parts and tools largely, she said, because she wouldn't have known what to do with them if she had them, especially when she first started riding. Consequently her contacts with mechanics all over the world were frequent and it was her conclusion that American repairmen—North American, that is—often were not too pleasant to deal with. "In the states they have their secret sanctuaries out in the back and they won't even allow you to look at what they're doing to your bike."

By contrast, in places like Mexico, Ecuador, Colombia, Peru, Australia and most of Europe, dealers and mechanics not only let her watch them work on her machine but often taught her how to make her own minor repairs. An exception to the American rule was two men in a Suzuki shop in Arizona who worked for six hours on her bike, then reluctantly accepted $6 after first saying they didn't want any money—"just wanted to help you on your way." Then the shop owner gave her a small timing light and taught her how to use it.

Also like many women bikers, Jan sort of drifted into motorcycling, finding it convenient and economical. In her case it began in Munich, Germany, in 1961 when she met a girl who had a motor scooter and who asked her to come along on a tour

Jan Gallagher's unique method of packing her bike breaks every rule in the book—but it works, for her.

of Europe. The scooter was stolen the second day out, and even though Jan had ridden only a short distance, and just as a passenger, the idea of two-wheeled transportation stayed with her when she went back to California. She bought her own scooter, but sold it when she joined the Peace Corps and was sent to Ecuador.

By the time she was ready to leave Ecuador she had agreed to sponsor a young student who wanted to come to the United States to study, and she figured the cheapest way to get them both back to the states would be on a motorcycle. So she bought a Suzuki 250, the student climbed on the back and they were off.

Neither Jan nor her friend knew anything about motorcycles, not even how to change a tire or fill the battery (they didn't even know where the battery was), but during their 6,000-mile ride they picked up a lot of tricks that might be useful to any more orthodox cross-country rider. For example, they always made room to pack an umbrella to provide shade during rest stops—not for themselves but for the bike. They learned to hitchhike by putting themselves and their machine in big trucks whose drivers took pity on them if road and weather conditions were bad.

Later, when she started her round-the-world trip, Jan perfected her unique method of loading her bike, which makes a joke of all accepted procedures.

"To carry most of my stuff," she said, "I had my grandmother's shopping cart tied to the back of my seat."

To this she added a Chinese wicker hamper lashed to the luggage carrier and extending about a foot out behind the rear wheel. With camping gear, clothing and food, topped by one and sometimes two guitars and her artist's painting materials, the whole load stuck up about three feet above her head.

"Whenever I see pictures of that thing, I always marvel at how I made it at all," she said.

She found that little string bags tied to the outside of the load were very handy for food snacks and small, frequently used items. Not a bad idea, even for a normally loaded bike.

Jan knew her machine was dangerously top-heavy ("I didn't even have saddlebags, so couldn't pack anything below seat level, until much later when a friend made me a pair out of canvas"), but she learned to drive accordingly. One thing worried her when she was traveling alone. If she parked the bike and it fell over, she wouldn't be able to pick it up without unloading it or waiting until someone came along to help.

On the whole, in cross-country riding Jan thinks "it's an advantage being a girl. Talk about getting help. I never took any equipment along for changing tires. I knew it would be beyond me anyway to get the tire off the rim, so I didn't even bother with the stuff."

But she also was very careful to replace tires when they showed the least signs of wear, with the result that her bike "has gone 38,000 miles and never had a flat tire in its life."

For women who wonder if it's better to travel alone or in pairs or groups, Jan said that it's up to the individual but that "traveling alone has its advantages." This surprised me until she explained: "If you like meeting different people and going into their homes and becoming part of their life and finding out about them, well, it happens a lot more if you're alone. People are going to think twice about walking up to two of you."

Another question I asked a lot of women bikers was whether they thought they were discriminated against because of their sex. Boiling down the answers, it seems that the majority don't feel that they are. One of them sort of shook me up for a moment when she said, "Yes, I do think I'm discriminated against for being a girl with a bike." Then she added, "But it's all good. I've gotten nothing but good service from gas stations and people on the streets when anything has happened."

Probably the typical answer was "No discrimination." Like the woman from New York who said she was "just accepted as a fellow biker . . . it's really nice to be treated as an equal." And another one said that with helmet, jacket, boots and all, nobody knew she was a woman riding alone until she stopped and shook out her curls and "started walking like a girl."

Freeda Fairbanks' first experience with the police may not have been typical—two veteran motorcycle cops taught her how to ride—but her response to my survey indicated that women's experiences with the police averaged out about the same as men's. To the question "Do you feel the police agencies you've dealt with are fair to bikers?" she replied:

"Very fair. Two years ago as a rank beginner—not even a bicycle rider—I was taught to ride by two motorcycle officers in Long Beach, California. I have never since been stopped by an officer. At the time of my one and only accident the officer was more than fair and very kind.

"There have been several times when I know I was saved an accident by using the recounted experiences of those two veteran policemen who taught me. It is my opinion that everyone should take such a course, no matter how well he may think he rides."

What she had to say makes good sense, no matter what sex you are.

A woman from the East Coast found that most police, especially New York state troopers, are friendly and understanding, but that "some small town police like to hassle you." Another stressed the fact that a rider's treatment depended mostly on how he or she acted and looked. The police, she said, "harassed the bums but were always nice to me and the other nice ones I know."

I'm not going to try to say much more about women bikers because Miss Fairbanks summed it all up when she wrote on the back side of the survey questionnaire:

"I cannot send a survey paper in such as this without appealing to other women to get out and find out what can be created just by doing your own thing on the highways.

"Few are such late-bloomers as I, starting to ride in what we call 'middle life.' I've gone from a 175 Enduro to a 350 Honda to a 650, and now to a 750 Yamaha—all in two years. Most of my 35,000 miles have been as a lone rider.

"I have treated others with consideration and have received the same usually. The image of arrogant non-consideration (on the part of motorists and others) is gradually being replaced with interest by non-riders.

"Women will find that most men do not resent your presence beside them on the highways, even if sometimes you ride a larger bike than they.

"So let's see more women try their wings on the open road as they are doing in the off-street areas. As they do this, the by-laws and rules of motorcycle clubs will change to make a place for even the single gal who wants to ride with the group."

16 / In The Women's Dorm

As long as we're on the subject of women, I might as well tell you about one of the more bizarre nights I spent while on my trip.

It had been a long, beautiful day, starting just outside the town of Aylmer in the province of Ontario. From there I traversed the rest of Ontario and crossed back into the United States at Niagara Falls.

I spent some time sightseeing at the Falls, then headed out through upstate New York, going along Highway 104 which skirts Lake Ontario but is two or three miles inland from the shore. The summer harvest apparently was in full swing and there were roadside fruit and vegetable stands just about everywhere I looked.

I arrived in Rochester about 5 P.M., just fifteen minutes too late to visit the Kodak Laboratories, which I had really wanted to see. I could have waited until the next day, but there was still good light for riding and I wasn't tired, so I went on through the evening. The sun was just disappearing, and the long twilight began as I pulled into Oswego. I didn't see anything interesting in the way of somewhere to stay, but I remembered passing a college campus on the outskirts of town and decided to go back and ask around for a good place to eat and spend the night.

The school was New York State University at Oswego, and I parked the bike and started strolling through the campus—a beautiful place perched on the shores of Lake Ontario. I must have been in some kind of a trance, drinking in the scenery in the quiet evening, not paying attention to where I was walking,

until I bumped into a girl coming out of one of the buildings. She was pretty, with long flowing blond hair and bright blue eyes.

I apologized and then explained I had just arrived in town and was looking for a good inexpensive place to get supper. She suggested the university cafeteria, and that sounded fine so I asked if she'd care to join me. She had just had her meal, and in fact was coming out of the cafeteria when I ran into her, but she agreed to have a cup of coffee and keep me company while I ate. She said her name was Cindy.

The cafeteria immediately brought back memories of my own college days. The long rows of tables, the food that always seemed to taste the same no matter what you ordered, and students busily talking or sitting in corners trying to get in some last-minute studying for an exam.

After we sat down I began telling Cindy about my trip and right away she was interested; she had never had a chance to do much traveling herself. When I got to the part about the Indians in Arizona she really perked up and began asking questions. She was a sociology major and one of her special interests was American Indians. She made me promise I'd send her a picture of the Navajo family after I got home.

After dinner we walked out to take a look at the motorcycle and Cindy wanted to go for a ride. I hated to tell her it was impossible but I had to—the machine was so loaded down there wasn't room for a passenger, and I couldn't unpack it because there was no place to leave all the stuff safely.

"No problem," she said brightly. "Just put your luggage in my room at the dorm."

This came as somewhat of a shock. In my college days not very many years before, a girls' dorm was inviolable. But times had changed, I realized, so we unloaded the bike and carried everything up to her room. By then it was around 9 P.M. and getting pretty cold out, so I told her to wear a heavy coat. I didn't have an extra helmet for her and could only hope we didn't get stopped by a policeman.

We took a road that followed the Lake Ontario shoreline and rode for a half-hour or so, when I figured I'd better get back and load up again and find a place to spend the night.

On the way up to the room we ran into Cindy's roommate, and after Cindy had introduced us, and told her about the ride, the roommate asked where I was going to sleep.

"Oh, didn't Cindy tell you?" I asked jokingly. "I'm staying here with you two."

"That's fine with me," she said.

"Wait a minute. I was only kidding."

But then Cindy spoke up: "Why don't you stay? All your things are here and there's no point in going out now and trying to find a place this late."

Well, if I was surprised before when Cindy asked me to put my gear in her room, I was really shaken up this time. When I was in college a short six years earlier you couldn't get near a women's dormitory in a Sherman tank. But now, I was given to understand, school regulations allowed all-night visiting privileges.

I must admit that when I had sort of reconciled myself to this new world it didn't take me long to make up my mind to stay. The room was small, about the same size as the one I'd had in college. Cindy and her roommate—I finally learned her name was Jane—had their beds against opposite walls with desks in between. The view from the window was spectacular, looking out over the lake.

Cindy and Jane had some studying to do and I spent the time chatting with some of their friends who dropped in. The rules may have changed in six years but students still had the same problems. One girl was complaining she had a test the following morning and still had two books to read. I remembered the feeling very well. Another protested she didn't have anything to wear to a dance Friday night and wondered if Cindy might have something she could borrow. All in all, that night brought back many fond memories of my school days.

Finally about 1 A.M. it was bedtime. I unrolled my sleeping bag on the floor near the foot of one of the beds and fell asleep thinking: "They'll never believe this back home."

17/ Visit To A Foreign Country: Canada

There was a funny thing about the route I took across the United States. At one point I actually saved time and mileage by going clear out of the country to get from one place to another.

You might have to look at a map to understand this, but the shortest distance from Detroit, Michigan to Buffalo, New York, is by way of Canada, skirting the northern shore of Lake Erie rather than looping down along the south shore.

I liked the idea of taking the bike into a "foreign country." It was romantic. Even though the first thing that greeted me just across the border was a Kentucky fried chicken stand. "Oh, God," I said to myself.

But right away things began to change when I got outside the city of Windsor and started through the countryside. Somehow or other, everything seemed a little older and mellower than in the United States. There weren't garish new filling stations at every corner. The ones I did see looked like they were twenty or thirty years old. The same was true of grocery stores and other small businesses. No supermarkets or sprawling shopping centers, more the "Mom and Pop" kind of thing. I liked it.

There was an old-fashioned air about it all. In the fields it looked like families, instead of a bunch of hired hands, were there working side by side—father, mother and children. When I thought about it I decided the best way to describe it all was to assume that Canada was about a generation behind America, and as far as I'm concerned I hope they never catch up.

The first night in Canada I spent in a campground just outside Aylmer where I met five Canadians whose tent was pitched next to mine. We had a chance to do a lot of talking and I got the impression from them that Canadians are very nationalistic, or patriotic, much more so than Americans. These five were students and I was very surprised that they expressed no desire to go across the border just a few miles away to visit the United States.

The next day I left Canada at Buffalo and then entered it again two days later below Montreal, not to save time and mileage but because I had a friend to visit in Montreal and because I was intrigued with what I had seen of the country. I'm glad I did it, because Montreal now ranks as one of my two favorite cities. (The other one is San Francisco.) It seems to be well-planned and has a new metro underground railway that makes travel easy. But at the same time much of an old-world flavor has been preserved.

I spent some time just walking around and found the people exceptionally friendly, like the man I stopped to ask a question. He took an hour and a half to show me some of his favorite places, and from him and some others I gathered that the citizens love their city, take great pride in it and enjoy telling others about it. That's pretty refreshing after being used to rather jaded or cynical Americans.

At one place in the downtown section I came across a band of sidewalk musicians. A large group of shoppers had stopped to listen, and suddenly a couple broke from the audience and started dancing while others began clapping and cheering. A cigarette that looked and smelled like marijuana was being passed around among about five or six of the audience, apparently without any fear of the law stepping in.

The second night in Montreal I visited the night club and coffeehouse part of town and found a great number of motorcycles pulled up along the curbs. There were quite a few Hondas like mine, but my bike seemed to attract a crowd right away. I soon found out the reason. Mine was the only one that had been customized. They told me that parts, especially for Hondas, were almost impossible to get, and they wanted to know all about prices and places to order from.

I stayed at what I guess would be called a rooming house instead of trying to find a campground in Montreal. There were a lot of similar places around the downtown areas. Mine cost $6 a night and was clean and pleasant and operated by friendly people. The accommodations weren't the most modern in the

world—the bathroom was down the hall—but after sleeping on the ground for quite a few nights anything seemed luxurious.

After three days I was ready to move on to New England, but everybody I talked to said I should first visit Quebec and they didn't have to press me too hard. I took a look at the map and figured it would be just as easy to cross into Maine from there as from Montreal. It was about a five-hour ride and I took off. The weather wasn't exactly the best I could have asked for and I had to hole up in coffee shops a couple of times to avoid thunder showers. The scenery, with the St. Lawrence River off to the right, would have been great if I could have looked at it.

I arrived in Quebec about 6 P.M. under partly cloudy skies, and I must say the first view of that magnificent city is breath-taking—broad avenues and statues and buildings with pillars, and trees along the sidewalks. I headed for the old section of town, which everyone had recommended.

That section, which I guess is about ten blocks square, is closed in by a stone wall about ten or twelve feet high, and when I got to the arched gateway there was a sign saying no motorcycles. When I asked some passers-by what it was all about, they told me that a couple of years before some motorcycle gangs had roared up and down the narrow streets of the old city, terrorizing everybody, so in order to stop that sort of thing all bikes were banned. But there was a designated area near the gate for parking motorcycles, so I left my machine there and spent about an hour walking around in the little cobblestoned streets, looking at the quaint shops and hassling with some panhandlers who I assumed were American hippie types because they spoke English while almost everybody else in town spoke French.

The language thing made me really feel like a world traveler, but it was a pain in the neck when I started trying to ask people where to find a place to stay for the night. I finally got a man who told me that if I wanted something inexpensive I should go to the old bastille, or jail. He said he wasn't kidding, but he also couldn't tell me how to get there. So I went back to my bike, and while I was trying to question people around the parking lot a man on a motorcycle came along and offered to lead me to the prison.

I followed him through the city and up a winding road until I spotted an old stone fortress through the trees. It looked exactly like what it was, the bastille.

For just fifty cents a night you can have your own jail cell to sleep in at the old bastille in Quebec.

Inside, the man behind an old desk told me I could have my own cell for just 50 cents a night. It really wasn't too bad, because they had old mattresses spread out all over the stone floors of the cells and you just unrolled your sleeping bag and there you were. And who could complain about the price? I was told it was open for travelers only during the summers because there was no heat.

The "jailer" said he would keep an eye on the belongings I unpacked, so I was able to ride back down to look around the city a little more. I was still having trouble finding people who spoke English, so after I parked the bike downtown and was walking around, listening to nothing but French for about an hour, I got all excited when I overheard a couple in front of me chatting away in my native tongue. This was a good excuse to introduce myself. They told me they were from a town in the province of Ontario and were just visiting about during their vacation.

We explored the narrow, twisting streets of the old city some more and at about 10 P.M. decided to ride the ferry across the St. Lawrence. The view from the middle of the river was fantastic, with the city spread out on the hillside.

We stayed on the ferry for the return trip and then I walked my new friends to the bus station and they left for home. I went back to my cell and was released the next morning to head for New England.

18 / Amish Country

It was a warm day with a light overcast sky and I was zipping along Highway 30 in southern Pennsylvania, near Lancaster, when up ahead I noticed something that looked very out of place.

It was a horse-drawn buggy with a man and two children inside. When I took a close look at the rig, I realized it was no stunt but rather must be the family's only mode of transportation.

The man and the children were dressed as if they had just stepped out of the 1900's. He was wearing a long black overcoat and a black felt hat, and the children were both dressed in black with high laced shoes. The boy wore suspenders on his pants and the girl had on an old-fashioned Ankle-length dress and a little bonnet.

I then realized I must be in Amish country. The Amish, I knew, are a sect of people who don't believe in newfangled contraptions or the modern way of life. They believe in living their lives as their ancestors did. They don't use any modern conveniences at all—automobiles, motorcycles or anything else run by a gasoline engine.

I really got a funny feeling driving through this area. I felt like I was entering a whole new country, with different customs, life style and morals. If you're in Pennsylvania it's worth going out of your way just to experience for a moment what life was like seventy-five years ago.

19 / New York City

Throughout my journey across the country I avoided big cities like the plague. I made a wide detour around Chicago, stayed completely away from Detroit, and just skimmed through the outskirts of Buffalo. Of course I didn't miss Montreal and Quebec; they were exceptions. The city I really wanted to stay away from was New York, but I had to go there because of business.

A motorcycle loaded down for cross-country travel is no vehicle for big-city traffic. Constant stops and starts overheat the engine and are tough on the clutch and transmission. It's difficult to make quick maneuvers. And, being a stranger in town, I figured I'd spend most of my time getting lost.

It was when I was in Montreal that I finally realized I was going to have to venture into New York. I had been in touch with my agent, who told me the editors wanted me to stop by in the city and talk over details of this book. So I had no choice and consoled myself with the knowledge I could visit a couple of friends while there.

I spent the night before I was due in New York in Provincetown, near the tip of Cape Cod. According to the map I had about a 300mile ride ahead of me so I got an early start, thinking that if traffic was anything like around Los Angeles I would need all the time I could get.

As I got closer to New York, the things I had heard about it made me more apprehensive—the natives were supposed to be unfriendly, the streets and traffic awful, and muggers were lurking behind every garbage can.

The weather was overcast when I started out, and by noon some intermittent sprinkles began hitting me. I was traveling by toll road because there didn't seem to be any easy scenic route available. In the early afternoon I was just easing along when a man on a BMW rode up beside me. His bike was fully loaded, indicating that he was a long-distance rider, too. We smiled at each other and tooled along side by side for a while, and finally I made hand signals asking if he'd like to stop for a drink. He nodded and we got off the road and found a small café. He told me that his name was Roger and that he was on his way home to Michigan after visiting friends in New England. We talked awhile over our coffees and decided to ride together for the last hundred miles.

Back on the road the weather was still gray and threatening, but the sprinkles had stopped and the miles passed pleasantly. Pretty soon we were on the outskirts of the Big City. We pulled off the road to get directions because neither of us knew exactly where to go next—except that Roger wanted to miss as much of the city as he could and head on west, while I had to find out how to get into the middle of town.

I don't remember the exact directions I got (they confused me then and they still do), but there was something about turning right on the last street before a bridge in order to get to the address I wanted. I think it was the Hell's Gate bridge. Whatever it was, it was a toll bridge. There was one problem: How would I know if that street I had just passed was the last one, or if there was one more? I could see the bridge up ahead but it was hard to tell if there was another street before I got to it. Well, there wasn't and I arrived at the tollgate and there was no place to turn around, even on a motorcycle. The attendant said all I could do was cross the bridge, get some new directions and come back.

So I went across into Queens and pulled into the first gas station I came to. It looked like a small independent station, kind of run down. Two men sat in front drinking beer. I pulled up near them and said I was trying to find an address over in Manhattan and asked if they could straighten me out.

"Don't get all worked up over nuthin'," one of them said. "Park your bike and relax a little and have a can of beer with us."

What's this? I asked myself. Everybody had told me people were tough and unfriendly and suspicious of strangers in New York, and here some guy in a grubby-looking gas station where

I'm not even going to buy a pint of gas is inviting me to sit down and drink a beer.

I rolled the bike over a little ways to park it and they saw the California license plate. Then the old familiar question popped out: "You didn't ride that thing all the way from California, did you?" For the hundredth time I answered, "Yeah, I sure did," and the questions started. Forty-five minutes and several beers later they gave me very detailed instructions on how to get where I wanted to go, and thanks to them I was back in Manhattan at my friend's house in less than fifteen minutes.

My first concern that night was what to do with my machine. I didn't want to leave it on the street because of all the rumors I'd heard about bike thieves, so I decided the best thing would be to find an overnight garage. The first two I tried said they wouldn't have anything to do with a motorcycle, and the third one agreed to let me keep it there for $3 but only on the condition I'd come and take it away by seven o'clock the next morning.

I was there on time the next day, and since I didn't have any

appointments until later in the afternoon I took off to explore the city. The first thing that struck me was that New York was amazingly well organized. I had no trouble finding addresses because the numbers of the various blocks were consistent. (My getting lost the night before was a sort of different matter.) And things seemed to be concentrated in a relatively small area. Anyone who has been around Los Angeles knows what I mean by this. Los Angeles sprawls all over the place and street numbers get mixed up, and in many places one street will have several different names in the space of a few blocks.

Then I was impressed with the feeling of intensity and excitement in the air, coming from all the people around me, scurrying along in all directions, each one seeming to be engaged on a serious mission and wasting no time going straight at it.

In spite of what I said about a loaded motorcycle being difficult to handle in city traffic, I found that in New York it was about the best way to get from place to place. The traffic is so bad I can't describe it—cars and taxis cutting each other off, delivery trucks double- or even triple-parked causing long-tie-ups. At least on the bike I was able to get around or through most of the obstacles. Not all, but most.

The street pavements themselves are absolutely horrendous, the worst I've seen anywhere. A rider has to watch constantly for chuckholes, and some of them seemed to be a foot or more deep. In almost every block, street crews were tearing up the pavement for some reason or other and of course had their barricades up.

But mostly my impressions of the city were favorable. Everyone I talked to was helpful and informative. The weather, at least during the three days I was there, was fine. Skies were blue and clear, there was no smog and the temperature was a pleasant 75 degrees. One person I talked to said they happened to be the best three days of the year.

One night when I was walking around I passed the Democratic head-quarters for George McGovern, and I figured that such an office in New York City should be pretty interesting. I went inside and it just happened to be the night when Mrs. Sargent Shriver, wife of the vice-presidential candidate, was there. She gave a short speech and departed, and after that I began talking to some of the volunteer workers. They were very informative and showed me what was going on

in the various offices and departments. But they couldn't hide the feeling that they were a little worried about their candidate's chances, no matter how they tried to portray outward confidence.

I didn't have much time to really go sightseeing around New York. I missed such places as the Village, Central Park and even the Statue of Liberty. But I was pleased with the little bit I did see and to go back—even if I can't pick the best three days of the year.

Since there are more cases of motorcycle thefts in the larger cities than in the more sparsely populated areas, if you do plan to visit a couple of those sprawling metropolitan areas, I suggest studying carefully the next chapter.

20/Preventing Theft

The theft and resale of hot motorcycles is a big business in the United States, amounting to millions of dollars in losses every year, and a biker should take every precaution he can think of or is told about to protect his machine and his belongings.

There are a number of devices on the market designed to thwart or at least discourage thieves. The oldest of these is the lock and chain, and for a long time this simple measure was pretty effective. A biker simply looped the chain through a wheel and around a tree or lamppost or parking meter, snapped the lock shut and felt secure.

But crooks keep up with developments, and before long they were using a good pair of bolt cutters and could get away with a bike in a matter of seconds. So motorcycle owners went to case-hardened steel chains and locks—and the thieves retaliated with cutting torches.

Then manufacturers started producing alarm systems and I think most of them are pretty effective. One is called Cycle-Guard and consists of a small unit that attaches to the bike on the license-plate bracket. It is so sensitive that an alarm sounds if anyone moves your machine even the slightest bit. The same manufacturer also has a more sophisticated model, the Cycle-Guard 2, which not only sets off the alarm on the bike but also transmits a signal to a small beeper box that you carry in your pocket and lets you know, even if you're several blocks away, that some one is messing with your machine. Many insurance companies are so impressed with the alarm devices that they lower your premiums if you have one.

On my bike I have the Cycle-Guard and a very heavy case-hardened chain and lock. I feel that between the two of them I've got about the best protection I can get.

But thieves, given a little time and some opportunity, can steal just about anything they determine on, regardless of what measures are taken to prevent them. So the next step toward peace of mind is theft insurance to cover both the bike and the gear you have packed on it.

Insurance rates vary from state to state and even from area to area. In Southern California, where the risk factor is considered to be exceptionally high, the theft insurance alone on my bike runs about $80 a year. Other forms of insurance on motorcycles, such as liability, fire, and protection against the uninsured motorist, seem to run a little lower than comparable coverage on automobiles and other vehicles. But again, rates also vary from company to company, so I advise shopping around. In my area of California the rates for complete coverage range anywhere from $140 to more than $300 a year.

Protecting the luggage on your bike is even more difficult than protecting the bike itself. If you can get everything into saddlebags, side cases or a scoot boot, all with locks on them, you can feel relatively good about walking away for a few minutes. But if you have a lot of stuff hung all around in the open, secured only by bungee cords, and maybe your helmet, goggles and gloves perched loose on the seat, don't stray too far for too long.

Of course, a lot will depend on where you are with regard to amount of traffic, type of neighborhood (residential or business) and lighting conditions if it's nighttime.

Quite often, if I wanted to go into a restaurant or browse around a main street, I'd ask a shopkeeper or someone else nearby if they would please keep on eye on the bike. Under other conditions, if I felt uneasy about leaving the machine I would just lift my saddlebags off and carry them with me; they were made with that in mind.

The main thing to remember is that the chance always exists that you will be ripped off. Keep this in mind every time you stop. Take the ignition key with you, use your chain and lock, activate your alarm system, throw your saddlebags over your shoulder.

Don't just walk away, all trusting, and invite some character to step in and ruin your whole trip in a couple of fast minutes.

Epilogue

Months after my cross-country trip was over and while I was in the midst of preparing this book, I took a day off and went down to the beach in Southern California. In the parking lot above the sand I saw two bikes with Wisconsin license plates. They were all packed for travel, and the two riders were just sitting there, straddling their seats, gazing at the Pacific Ocean for the first time—and at the bikinis.

They were Dale Prahl and Greg Hahn, both twenty-one and both from Wausau, Wisconsin, and they had been on the road about ten days. They looked a little sunburned and their hair was matted (they had taken off their helmets for a while when they found they weren't required to wear them in California). Both were riding Triumphs, Dale's a stock 500 and Greg's a 650 with a pretty drastically extended front end. Neither had a fairing but both their helmets had face shields. They were looking for a place to camp that night, with showers.

At least I could provide the showers, so we went up to my house for a while. Since I couldn't put them up for the night, I phoned a campground down the coast near the Western White House and made arrangements for them. Then, when they were all showered and combing out their wet hair and drinking a beer, we talked about motorcycling.

Both of them had lived all their lives within a few miles of their homes in rural Wisconsin. Both were going to go to trade technical schools in the fall. Both had secure safe lives ahead of them, surrounded by solid families. Neither could have afforded this trip by any means except bikes.

They talked about the 3,700 miles they had covered so far,

the camps they had stayed in. They had been impressed and even a little awed "by the whole country, by all the states that seemed to be different, not just in names but in scenery."

And then Dale, swishing the beer in his can, said what so many other cross-country bikers say:

"It's more than the country. It's the people you meet. My family wanted me to stay around. Everything was there. A way of life. But I had to get out, just once, and see and meet other people. At first they all seemed different too, like the scenery, but I found after a little while, when I had a chance to talk and listen, that people everywhere are much the same as me."

Appendix

Appendix

Survey Results
Usually I'm not very much influenced by polls and surveys. But when two of them, conducted entirely independently, come up with a lot of the same answers, I've got to admit I'm impressed.

The fact that one of them was my own might have something to do with it.

The other survey was taken by the national magazine *Road Rider* in 1971. Mine was conducted a whole year later and this time lapse produced some interesting variations in the results. For one thing, it indicated that more and more women seem to be taking to cross-country riding.

Road Rider's readership is made up almost entirely of cross-country bikers, and since the people I questioned were practically all long-distance riders, too, the two surveys have a good basis for comparison.

I didn't have a magazine subscription list to poll for my survey, so when I was planning my trip I decided the best thing I could do was to have questionnaires printed up for distribution to bikers I met on the road. To encourage them to be sure and send me their answers, I gave each of them a stamped envelope.

The forms came back from a pretty impressive cross-section of bikers from all parts of the United States (and even a couple from Canada), ranging in age from sixty-one down to seventeen. The age spread didn't surprise me, but what did strike me was the fact that 50 percent of them were between twenty-eight and forty-five. I had expected the average age to be lower.

One question concerned the type of bike used, and exactly one-third, or 33.3 percent, said Honda—either the 450, 500 or

750, with the majority on the big 750. Harley-Davidson was next at 28 percent, and again the majority favored the bigger models like the 1200 displacement job, rather than the smaller sportsters.

In third place was the German-made BMW, with 22 percent. This so-called "Rolls-Royce of the road machines" is popular because it is quiet and smooth, largely since it has a drive shaft rather than a chain.

Suzuki, which was just beginning to be recognized in the cross-country field with its reliable 750 water-cooled two-stroke engine, rated 7.4 percent.

The remaining 9.3 percent rode such bikes as Jawa, Norton, Triumph, Moto Guzzi, Kawasaki and Yamaha.

I was very impressed by the length of individual trips taken by some of those who responded to the poll. About one-twelfth of them said 10,000 miles or more was not unusual for a single journey, and more than 26 percent said their longer rides were between 5,000 and 10,000 miles. About 16 percent traveled between 3,000 and 5,000 miles, followed by 21 percent going between 2,000 and 3,000 miles.

To me this indicates a lot of serious cross-country riding by people with a lot of experience in covering long distances. I think this lends real weight to their answers in other categories.

For example, the answers to "Do you feel the police agencies you've dealt with are fair to bikers?" were especially interesting to me because like everyone else I had heard many rumors about police going out of their way to hassle motorcyclists. The survey seemed to prove that most of the unpleasant stories were just that—stories. Here are some typical answers:

"Yes, very fair in all ways. Once in Virginia City, when Hell's Angel types were reported coming into the area, the sheriff directed us to put our bikes at the courthouse under his guard."

From Los Angeles: "I have had no bad experiences with the police. I have found them friendly and extremely helpful."

From Lawrence, Kans.: "Yes. They have told me many times where I could sleep in or around a town when I couldn't find a camp site."

From Dana Point, Cal.: "Yes. I have never been harassed or stopped without cause. Have found excessive noise attracts more police attention than 10 miles over the speed limit."

Another Californian wrote that he has "never (knock on wood) received a ticket, although I generally travel at 80 or more miles per hour on the road. I have been stopped five or six times, two of which were because the policeman only wanted to tell me my taillight was out!"

My question "What are some of the more interesting experiences you've had while riding?" brought a type of answer I really didn't expect because I was thinking in terms of weird happenings and odd adventures and maybe even bad accidents. But a biker from Mississauga, Ontario, spoke for the majority: "I got caught in a tornado once in the middle of the night, but the people you meet are THE experience."

A Southern California rider waxed poetic: "Sunrises, sunsets. The sights and smells of the open country. Talking with people I meet on the road."

And they went on like that—"the people you meet," "talking to people," "finding out what other people think about," "getting into people's homes and getting into their lives," "learning about people."

It got to the point where I went into a sort of idealistic trance thinking that maybe motorcycles would be the instrument for bringing people closer together where a lot of more sophisticated approaches had failed. A pleasant dream, maybe not too far-fetched if the two-wheelers and the four-wheelers put a little effort into it.

I asked another question, a little bit like the one above but aimed at finding out if the overall image of motorcyclists is improving after the bad reputation they got during the 1950's and 60's from outlaw gangs and sensational movies. I asked bikers to report on any bad experiences they had had just because they rode motorcycles.

The majority reported they had had none, but it's worth mentioning the few exceptions. Their main complaint was about discourteous or unobservant automobile drivers, and one or two seemed to have encountered people who just plain tried to run them off the road.

A biker from Miami said his only bad experience came from drivers who "cut in front of me on purpose." I think this is a problem all bikers are aware of, but if you're driving safely and anticipating such moves you'll come out all right.

One rider, from Ouray, Colorado, started out by saying, "Seeing different parts of the country is my biggest experience," but he also said that "people in cars liked to play with me along the road, cutting in and out, forcing me over." Then, however, he sort of let me know what kind of guy he was by adding: "I like riding without hands, leaning back against the sleeping bag." I hope he lives long enough to read this.

A cyclist from Santa Ana, California, wrote: "I've had very few bad experiences, but the ones I have had are mostly because of pre-existing ideas that all bikers are Hell's Angels types, no matter how you dress. I've never been refused service by anyone because I was a biker, although I know of several places that wouldn't have given me reservations if they had known in advance."

From Arlington, Virginia, a man wrote he had had only one bad experience in twelve years of riding. "A man in a pickup truck intentionally ran me off the road to show off to his girl friend."

A biker from Bloomington, Minnesota, said he was refused service at two gas stations, one in Montana and one in Wyoming, and a ranger threatened to kick him out of a national park "because I was a motorcycle bum."

Road Rider, which made its survey in July of 1971, was kind enough to let me quote some of the findings. Its poll was a bit more extensive than mine. I was pleased to see how closely our statistics matched. For example, 31.9 percent of their readers rode Hondas; my figure was 33.3 percent. Just as in my survey, theirs put Harley-Davidson in second place with 16.6 percent as compared to my 28 percent, and both surveys came up with BMW's in third place.

Under the category of accessories, both of us showed that most riders favor fairings or windshields (Road Rider, 47.4 percent; me, 57.4 percent). And both indicated that saddlebags are extremely popular (*Road Rider,* 41.3 percent; me, 49 percent).

I found the most intriguing category had to do with women riders. Because our surveys were so consistent in other areas, I believe I really uncovered a trend. Remember, there was a whole year between the two polls, and in 1971 when *Road Rider* asked the questions they found that only 2.78 percent of cross-country bikers were women. I got back a return of 7.4 percent, and I'm convinced that this shows women definitely taking to motorcycle travel in growing numbers.

Some other *Road Rider* statistics covered occupation and education of riders, with 25 percent listing their work as professional, 23.8 percent as laborers, 13.5 percent as self-employed, and 9.5 percent as tradesmen, with some executives, students, housewives, military personnel and retired persons making up the remainder.

On education, 40.3 percent were at or under high school level; 19.2 percent were college graduates; more than 25 percent had some college credits; 5.9 percent had a master's degree, and 2.5 percent a doctorate.

I believe these two surveys pretty well prove that people from all walks of life, from different backgrounds and in different age groups, and certainly in both sexes, are turning to motorcycles for their long-distance vacations.

At the same time, by their conduct and their approach to other people, they are slowly but surely wiping out the idea that a motorcycle is a symbol of gang violence and terror in whatever community it appears.

On pages 137 and 138 is a copy of the survey I distributed across the country. Sometime in the future I hope to update this book and would appreciate it if as many of you as possible could take the time to fill out the questionnaire and send it to me:

Vince Streano
c/o Random House
201 E. 50th St.
New York, N.Y. 10022

Motorcycle Laws
During my cross-country trip, while going through Illinois, I met a biker from Vermont. We were both going east: he to get home after touring the West Coast, I on my way to visit his part of the country. It was a casual meeting along the road and we stopped to have a cup of coffee and gossip.

He had been all across the country and halfway back, and one of the things that stuck most in his mind was the inconsistencies in state laws governing motorcyclists. He told me he had crossed the state line into Oregon and had gone about twenty miles when a highway patrolman pulled him over because he didn't have his headlight on—in broad daylight. It seems there is a law in Oregon that requires motorcyclists to keep their lights on at all times, day and night. He argued with the officer but it got him nowhere, even though he insisted he had never heard of such a law. He got a ticket.

As a matter of fact, at this writing there are nine states in which it is illegal to ride without a headlight burning twenty-four hours a day. At least two more states are considering a similar regulation, and in California twenty-four-hour headlights will be mandatory after January 1, 1975.

The use of headlights is not the only area in which the fifty states take different views, despite the fact that when you're riding through the continental United States you often can cross a state line without knowing it and come under entirely different regulations that wouldn't have affected you a few feet the other side of the line.

For example, assuming you wanted to go from California to New York and you wanted to obey the laws of each state, you could start out in California without a helmet. But the state line would be as far as you could go, because Oregon, Nevada and Arizona require helmets. You couldn't even sneak down through Mexico and hope to come back into the states and continue eastward, because the other border states, New Mexico and Texas, also require them.

So you buy a helmet and put it on and try to get out of California again, but you don't have eye protection such as goggles or a windshield. Well, you could go out through Oregon on the north, turn east through Idaho, Wyoming, Nebraska and Iowa. But that's as far as you could go.

The same confusion reigns when it comes to special licenses for cyclists, rear-view mirrors, footrests (pegs) for passengers, passenger seats and safety inspections. Some states require 'em and some don't. In Wyoming all you need is a safety inspection; in the other states you must meet anywhere from two to eight different requirements.

What to do about it? One way would be to conform to all the regulations regardless of which state you were in, which would mean:

Questionnaire

Dear fellow biker,

The following is a survey on cross-country motorcycle riders for an upcoming magazine article. If you ride your bike on the street and enjoy going places and would like to be a part of the survey, please complete the following questions in as much detail as possible. Thank you for your help.

Name _____ Age _____ Phone _____

Address _____ City _____ State _____ Zip _____

Make, model and year of motorcycle _____ approx. miles _____

What accessories or customizing is on your bike?

What major problems, if any, have you had with your bike?

What camping equipment do you carry on trips?

What spare parts do you carry while on bike trips?

What's the longest trip you've taken on your bike?

What area have you ridden through that you would recommend to other bikers?
(Please be specific, i.e.: towns, specific areas, highways, etc.)

What are some areas you definitely would NOT recommend to other bikers? Why?

Have you had any bad experiences from people because you're a biker?
Please explain.

What are some of the more interesting experiences you've had while riding?

Do you feel the police agencies you've dealt with are fair to bikers? Why?

- You'd wear a helmet and so would your passenger.
- Your headlight would be on at all times.
- You'd have a special driver's license, and you'd carry your ownership papers on the bike at all times.
- There'd be a seat for your passenger.
- Your passenger would have foot pegs.
- You'd have goggles or a windshield.
- You'd have a rear-view mirror.
- You'd have a safety inspection certificate.

On top of that, you'd never ride two abreast because some states don't allow it.

There's nothing wrong with following all these regulations. They're all designed to help ensure your own safety and that of your passenger.

But let's face it, it's confusing. Our hope lies in the early adoption of the Federal Highway Safety Program Standard No. 3 which eventually will make all states conform to the maximum safety standards—with the exception of burning the headlight at all times. Personally, as I've said, I'm in favor of burning mine anyway.

Following is a chart of States showing requirements in each state as of May 1972:

Motorcycle Requirements by States

State	Special Driver License	Safety Helmet	Eye Protect.	Passenger		Mirror Required	Safety Inspection	
				Seat	Foot-rests		At Time of Reg.	Period-ically
ALABAMA	X—A	X		X				
ALASKA	X—B	X	X	X	X	X		
ARIZONA	X	X	X	X	X	X		
ARKANSAS		X	X	X	X		X	X
CALIFORNIA	X			X	X	X		X—C
COLORADO	X	X	X			X	X	X
CONNECTICUT	X	X	X	X	X	X		X—C
DELAWARE	X—F	X	X	X	X	X	X	X
FLORIDA		X	X	X	X	X	X	X
GEORGIA	X	X	X	X	X	X	X	X
HAWAII	X	X	X	X	X	X	X	X
IDAHO		X		X			X	X
ILLINOIS	X		X	X	X	X		
INDIANA		X	X	X	X	X	X	X
IOWA				X	X	X	X—G	
KANSAS		X	X	X	X	X	X	
KENTUCKY	X	X	X	X	X	X	X	X
LOUISIANA	X	X	X	X	X	X	X	X
MAINE	X	X		X	X	X		X
MARYLAND	X	X	X	X	X	X		
MASSACHUSETTS	X	X		X	X	X	X	X
MICHIGAN	X	X	X—H			X		
MINNESOTA	X	X		X	X	X		
MISSISSIPPI						X		X
MISSOURI	X	X					X	X
MONTANA	X			X	X	X		
NEBRASKA	X	X						X
NEVADA	X	X	X	X	X	X		
NEW HAMPSHIRE	X	X	X	X	X	X		
NEW JERSEY	X	X	X	X	X	X	X	X
NEW MEXICO	X	X—I	X	X	X	X		X
NEW YORK	X	X	X	X	X	X	X	X
NORTH CAROLINA		X		X		X	X	X
NORTH DAKOTA	X	X		X	X	X	X	
OHIO	X	X	X	X	X	X		
OKLAHOMA	X—J	X—K	X	X	X	X		X
OREGON	X	X				X		X—C
PENNSYLVANIA	X	X	X	X	X			X
RHODE ISLAND	X	X	X	X	X			X
SOUTH CAROLINA	X	X	X	X	X	X		X
SOUTH DAKOTA	X	X	X	X	X	X		X
TENNESSEE	X	X	X	X	X	X		
TEXAS	X	X				X		X
UTAH	X	X—M	X—M	X	X		X	X
VERMONT	X	X	X	X	X	X	X	X
VIRGINIA	X	X	X	X	X	X	X	X
WASHINGTON	X	X	X	X	X	X	X—N	
WEST VIRGINIA	X		X			X		X
WISCONSIN	X	X	X	X	X	X		
WYOMING						X	X	X
DIST. OF COL.	X	X	X	X	X	X	X	X

Lights On All Times	Handlebar 15" Ht. Limit	Riding Prohibited			State
		Two Abreast	Between Lanes	Side-Saddle	
	X		X	X	ALABAMA
	X	X	X		ALASKA
					ARIZONA
X					ARKANSAS
X—D	X—E		X	X	CALIFORNIA
			X	X	COLORADO
	X	X	X	X	CONNECTICUT
	X		X	X	DELAWARE
X	X		X	X	FLORIDA
X	X		X	X	GEORGIA
			X	X	HAWAII
	X		X	X	IDAHO
X	X		X	X	ILLINOIS
X	X	X	X	X	INDIANA
	X		X	X	IOWA
	X		X	X	KANSAS
			X	X	KENTUCKY
	X		X	X	LOUISIANA
	X			X	MAINE
	X	X	X	X	MARYLAND
	X	X	X	X	MASSACHUSETTS
	X		X	X	MICHIGAN
	X—E		X		MINNESOTA
					MISSISSIPPI
	X				MISSOURI
X			X	X	MONTANA
					NEBRASKA
	X		X	X	NEVADA
	X			X	NEW HAMPSHIRE
	X		X	X	NEW JERSEY
	X			X	NEW MEXICO
X	X	X	X	X	NEW YORK
			X		NORTH CAROLINA
		X	X	X	NORTH DAKOTA
	X	X	X	X	OHIO
	X—L		X	X	OKLAHOMA
X					OREGON
	X				PENNSYLVANIA
	X				RHODE ISLAND
	X		X	X	SOUTH CAROLINA
	X	X	X	X	SOUTH DAKOTA
				X	TENNESSEE
			X	X	TEXAS
	X—E	X	X	X	UTAH
	X				VERMONT
	X	X	X		VIRGINIA
	X		X	X	WASHINGTON
	X		X	X	WEST VIRGINIA
X	X		X	X	WISCONSIN
			X		WYOMING
	X	X		X	DIST. OF COL.

A. Required if under 16
B. Required after July 1, 1973
C. Random Vehicle Inspection
D. Required after Jan. 1, 1975
E. Hand grips must be below shoulder height
F. Endorsement on license
G. First registration after sale
H. Required for speeds over 35 mph
I. Operators & passengers under 18
J. 14-16 years old restricted as to hours, speed and horsepower
K. Operators & passengers under 21
L. Height limit 12 inches
M. On roads with speed limits over 35 mph
N. At time of special endorsement on license

About the Author Vince Streano

was staff photographer for the Los Angeles Times from January 1968 to June 1973. A native Californian, he began his photography career while still in high school by working for a local paper as a lab assistant. In January 1968 he graduated from San Jose State University with a B.A. in journalism and went to work for the Times just two weeks later. His photos have won a number of local, state and national awards, and he is illustrator of three children's books published by the Children's Press in Chicago.

He is currently free-lancing in Southern California after completing a four-month tour on the Chapman College World Campus Afloat, where he was the ship's photographer and photography instructor.